INTERVENTIONS

Interventions is produced on the land of the Wurundjeri people of the Kulin Nation. We acknowledge the Traditional Owners of country throughout Australia and recognise their continuing connection to land, waters and culture. We pay our respects to their Elders past, present and emerging. Their land was stolen, never ceded. It always was and always will be Aboriginal land.

First published 2005 by Red Rag Publications
2nd edition 2024 by Interventions Inc

Interventions Inc is a not-for-profit, independent, radical book publisher.
For further information:

    www.interventions.org.au
    Info@interventions.org.au
    PO Box 24021
    Melbourne 3001

Title: United We Stand: Class Struggle in Colonial Australia
Author: Tom O'Lincoln

ISBN: 978-0-6452535-7-3: Paperback
ISBN: 978-0-6486416-0-5: ebook

Cover design of this edition by Stephanie Grigg
Design and layout of interior of this edition by Viktoria Ivanova
Front cover image: Eight hours day procession, Melbourne 1895 (State Library of Victoria).
Back cover image: Cartoon depicting women assaulting strikebreakers, Broken Hill strike 1892 (Outback Archives, Broken Hill City Library, NSW).

© Tom O'Lincoln 2005

The moral rights of the author have been asserted.
All rights reserved. Except as permitted under the Australian Copyright Act 1968 (for example, a fair dealing for the purposes of study, research, criticism or review), no part of this book may be reproduced, stored in a retrieval system, communicated or transmitted in any form or by any means without prior written permission.

All inquiries should be made to the publisher.

A catalogue record for this work is available from the National Library of Australia

CLASS STRUGGLE IN COLONIAL AUSTRALIA

Tom O'Lincoln

CONTENTS

Publisher's foreword to 2024 edition	i
Preface	iii
Introduction to 2005 edition	1
1: Our infant might: Working class struggle before the gold rushes	3
2: A power in the land: Australian unions, 1855–1890	29
3: Crisis and incorporation: Labour in the 1890s	55
4: Gender, class and the road to women's suffrage	81
5: Race, class and the road to White Australia	107
Endnotes	131
Bibliography and further reading on colonial Australia	143
Image Credits	155
Index	157

PUBLISHER'S FOREWORD TO 2024 EDITION

This book was first published in 2005 with the support of the Jeff Goldhar Project. It was the culmination of both a smaller and a bigger project. Tom O'Lincoln initially wrote a number of shorter essays on Australian history, which he published on his website, now sadly defunct. These essays were part of a larger and ambitious project – to write an entire history of Australian class struggle from a Marxist political perspective. However, the larger project proved problematic, and Tom decided to publish the present short history of class struggle in the pre-federation period as a standalone study.

There has been no attempt to update the content. The new edition retains the original text with very few alterations. We have made a small number of improvements to expression and some minor corrections. We have recognised modern language conventions – particularly about oppressed groups – and changed some wordage which might not be clear to a younger audience. Spelling and punctuation now accord with Interventions' style. We have modernised all references to Indigenous people where they occur in the text. How to handle potentially objectionable quotes can be a debatable subject; however, we at Interventions choose not to edit actual quotes. We leave them as they are, unless there is ambiguity. We have retained this practice in the present volume.

An important enhancement in the new edition is the inclusion of a preface by Terry Irving. Tom read it not long before he died; he was heartened and moved by Terry's appreciation of his contribution to Australian labour history.

This edition has also been enhanced by using graphics and photos from the period.

Many people provided comments or assisted in other ways in the two editions of this book. We would like to express our gratitude to: Mick Armstrong, Phil Griffiths, Tom Gilchrist, Steph Grigg, Eris Harrison, Tess Lee Ack, Rick Kuhn, Dougal McNeil, Simon O'Neil, Liz Ross, Jerome Small, Janey Stone, Ian Syson, Les Thomas, Jane Tovey and Phillip Whitefield.

PREFACE

While Tom O'Lincoln was writing *United We Stand*, I was writing *The Southern Tree of Liberty*[1] – each of us working within the tradition of Marxist history but unaware of what the other was doing. Our books appeared at about the same time, mine a little earlier than his, so it contained no acknowledgment of his book and the contribution it makes to radical history. Writing this preface to the new edition, therefore, gives me a welcome opportunity to do that.

United We Stand is an important book for three main reasons. Firstly, it is not a narrowly focused academic monograph, but a general history covering more than a century of working-class politics. The second is its provenance: it was written from within the working-class movement. It is the first book of this kind since Brian Fitzpatrick's *Short History of the Australian Labour Movement*[2] to be able to claim this distinction. Thirdly, and most importantly, because this book comes out of the socialist left of the working-class movement, its organising idea, as its title reveals, is class struggle. Let me suggest why this makes his book uniquely valuable.

Writing about class in history, and writing about class struggle in history, are not quite the same thing. Each is useful, but class struggle history has a political purpose. It must start with (or at least concentrate on) the specifics of contention and, in the process, reveal the principle of agency and the *excitement* generated when people take control of their lives.

The distinction I'm getting at is one that we are more likely to understand if we are already involved in struggle – or if we are seeking reasons to get involved. We will know immediately that histories of how people have been exploited and oppressed, and how they have been represented in history, are not exactly what we want. Yes, such studies are interesting (although sometimes dispiriting); they might even be valuable for the ammunition they provide for current campaigns. But, in the end, they don't inspire us to action. This, in a nutshell, is why I like Tom O'Lincoln's book. It's about working men and women, in particular situations, standing up and taking action. It succeeds in inspiring as well as informing us. This is the purpose of radical history.

On the matter of inspiration: I don't mean that it can be communicated through 'ra-ra' phrases. What I mean is that militants are inspired by discovering in history the experiences of the people in their struggles, their grit and creativity, their foibles as well as their heroism. In Tom O'Lincoln's book, we get many glimpses of that lived experience. In his discussion of the 1882–83 Tailoresses' Strike, using details from Rae Frances's study of the strike, he tells us that the women 'broke out of their conventional roles' and caused the accepted order of things to shudder. Reading about these events, we can almost hear the women swearing and threatening violence against the scabs. We can feel the employers' disbelief and affront that these women no longer had faith in male authority. In struggle, these women had discovered their agency; they broke class and gender rules; they scared the ruling class shitless. That's inspiring.

Of course, there's more to the book than stirring stories; it has a serious intent. It is meant to validate a particular theory of working-class politics. The theory starts from the proposition that, when workers form as a class, their role in history is to overthrow capitalism. As they become a class, they take a critical step when they form unions. Even more importantly, the workers and their unions need to develop an anti-capitalist political consciousness. For this, they need guidance from revolutionaries. That's it, in very general terms, omitting (for want of space) the manifold debates about strategy and tactics and the many studies of the overwhelmingly hostile environment in which the struggle takes place.

I grew up accepting this model of working-class politics, and for good reasons. Gaining strength in the first decades of the 20th century, it explained the Russian Revolution of 1917 and the progress of working-class communism into the middle of the century. In this period, a mood of triumphalism swept over parts of the left, and one of its effects was to rewrite the past of the working class as if it were always moving towards its triumph. Eric Hobsbawm called it a belief in 'the forward march of labour',[3] a belief that produced a submerged teleology in the first wave of academic labour history. If there were defeats and retreats, they arose because of the immaturity of the class. Another effect was to sideline any expressions of class politics that could not easily be assimilated to the unions–party–revolution model. Much of the history of working-class politics was simply brushed aside. These shortcomings were a legacy of focusing on the 'classical' or standard employment relationship of the 'Western' labour movement and ignoring, among other things, precarious employment, forced labour, domestic labour, self-employment and the porous boundaries between them and wage labour.

I am thinking about these issues because, since the publication of Tom O'Lincoln's book, and mine, new evidence about 19th century working-class politics in Australia has become available. It appears in two books by Michael Quinlan, *The Origins of Worker Mobilisation: Australia 1788–1850*[4] and *Contesting Inequality and Worker Mobilisation: Australia 1851-1880*.[5] Quinlan starts with a series of propositions: that workers have been coming together since the inception of capitalism; that their collective impulse arises because of the inequalities of power and resources in the capitalist labour process; that worker mobilisation is a window into the formation of the class; and that many of the expressions of collective action will be informal and ephemeral.

Through painstaking research over three decades, Quinlan produced a unique data base of instances of collective action, including strikes (many informally organised), court actions, go-slows, demonstrations, mass absconding, sabotage, petitions, political meetings, mutual insurance schemes and the formation of unions, peak labour bodies and political organisations. The scale is startling. For the period up to 1850, he made separate files for over 6,800 instances; from 1850 to 1880, more than 5,000. I said when reviewing the first of these books[6] that, although Michael Quinlan never intended his project to be a history of class struggle, it does provide us with the raw data that can make class struggle history more inclusive and less teleological. Noting the peaks and troughs, the transition points and the persistence of informal actions, we will be armed with new questions to ask and different forms and combinations of anti-capitalist politics to evaluate.

The last two chapters of Tom O'Lincoln's book move outside its chronological framework to take up the themes of racism and sexism in the 19th century. They show the value of a perspective framed by the needs of the movement – and the power of class analysis in the study of race and gender. They provide a much-needed corrective to the dominant view in academia that the labour movement was responsible for Australian sexism and racism.

A final reflection: as Quinlan contemplated what he had discovered about 19th century working-class mobilisation, he characterised it as a period of experimentation. As we contemplate the present demobilised state of working-class politics and ask questions about reviving class struggle, we might conclude that we don't have all the answers but that we do have a history full of experiments.

PREFACE

At the beginning of his book, Tom O'Lincoln declared that it would be a partisan history. The last sentence in the book exhorts us to write our own history. *United We Stand* shows us how to do that, using scholarly methods but with revolutionary intent.

Dr Terence H. Irving
Honorary Professorial Fellow
University of Wollongong

September 2023

INTRODUCTION TO 2005 EDITION

*We cannot choose our past;
that is given. But we can choose our history,
for history is part of the present.*

– Ian Turner[1]

The choices we make aren't innocent. When Prime Minister John Howard attacked the 'black armband' view of history in 1996, he was using an argument about history to attack Aboriginal and Torres Strait Islander Land Rights, Asian immigration and 'political correctness'. Two years later, as the labour movement mobilised to defend the Maritime Union of Australia in 1998, workers appealed to historical arguments of a different kind: they spoke, wrote and sang about workers' solidarity. To choose our history is to take sides. This book is partisan, its starting point much like the one pioneering labour historian Brian Fitzpatrick expressed in 1940:

> The history of the Australian people is amongst other things
> the history of a struggle between the organised rich and
> the organised poor, and the usual aim of the belligerents
> has been to keep or win political and economic power in
> order to use it in what they have considered to be their own
> interests. And I suppose no sensible person, whether of

the Right or Left, will quarrel with me on that score. But I discriminate between the belligerents. I take the view that the effort of the organised working class has been...an effort to achieve social justice.[2]

A decade or two ago, these words might have sounded quaint. 'Everyone knew' class politics was out of date. Yet, today, everyone knows that social inequalities are widening, and that governments and employers are systematically attacking unions and the rights of working people. Fear of the sack, stress at work, arrogant bosses and welfare cutbacks are everyday news. We need to fight back; and that's class struggle – so a book about class conflict in Australian history should be timely. The first three chapters recount the history of Australian trade unionism up to federation.

However, other objections to Fitzpatrick's outlook are less easily dealt with. His optimistic view, shared by other leftist historians of his era, tended to ignore or play down the entrenched sexism and racism that infected the labour movement. In more recent decades, 'New Left' and feminist historians have raised important challenges. Wasn't organised labour a 'men's movement'? Wasn't it the most important force supporting the White Australia policy?

While accepting some of their critique, I have also contested some of the New Left and feminist views. We can't brush aside sexism and racism the way an older generation of labour historians did, but neither should we place all the blame on the labour movement. The final two chapters argue for a new perspective on these questions.

Tom O'Lincoln
February 2005

1.
OUR INFANT MIGHT

WORKING CLASS STRUGGLE BEFORE THE GOLD RUSHES

In the state-run prison that was early New South Wales (NSW), pockets of capitalism sprang up quickly, like sturdy weeds.[1]

The Rum Corps' notorious officers turned the colony's administration upside down to screw personal profits out of convict labour. Their commander, Francis Grose, granted land to officers and assigned convicts to work for them, making the convict system a way to accumulate private capital. By 1800, these scoundrels were selling half the colony's grain. Their monopoly of armed force gave them a stranglehold on trade – including in rum, which for a time became the currency in NSW. Still not satisfied, they plundered public funds. When the Rum Corps lost power, new Governor Lachlan Macquarie fixed the worst abuses; but, essentially, their system remained, to be plugged into the vast, throbbing engine of Britain's market economy.

Where there's capitalism, there must be wage labour; and, where wage labour appears, class struggle is never far away.

When did Australian workers begin to unite? We are apt to date the origins of the Australian labour movement to the 1850s. In reality, workers were fighting back much earlier. In fact, signs of worker organisation appeared among the convicts – who were not really slave labour because, from shortly after the First Fleet landed until at least 1820, some of their time was their own.

The officers limited convicts' 'government hours' so that they could work extra time for wages. Having seized large tracts of land, the officers had an incentive to allow this: 'the settlers' fields, granted for nothing, were crying out for labour, and there was no labourer but the convict.'[2] No doubt, they would have preferred not to pay. But the convicts showed such determined sluggishness in performing unpaid labour that the officers had little choice. Governor Hunter's attempts to reverse these concessions were largely ignored. By 1798, he had fallen back on attempts to peg wages.

Generally, convicts were paid by the piece, but Hunter set 10 pence as a sort of daily going rate. Free labourers got an additional 2 pence. 'Mechanics' (skilled workers) commanded higher pay than the unskilled. These were the official rates; actual pay could be two to five times as much, depending on supply and demand. The ticket-of-leave system provided further possibilities. Originally intended to reduce the numbers receiving government rations, tickets-of-leave were later used as rewards for good behaviour. Either way, they opened up the labour market.

From the 1820s, convicts' rights were scaled back – as Commissioner Bigge recommended. He wanted to make transportation more of a deterrent back in Britain. Bigge also backed the colonial landowners, saw the potential to extract big profits out of the pastoral industry and, consequently, proposed a turn away from public farming with a greater emphasis on assignment. Convicts were prevented from bringing capital to the colony, and emancipists no longer received grants of land after 1825. We should not, however, contrast a cruel Bigge with a kinder

Macquarie. The governor himself had tried to limit the wages of convicts to £10 per year for males, £7 for females. (The Sydney elite complained that this was still excessive: they thought £3 or £4 quite sufficient.) Tighter discipline for convicts of both genders followed the construction of permanent prison buildings around 1819–20, *before* Bigge's recommendations could take effect.

In the following decades, under hardliners like Darling in NSW and Arthur in Van Diemen's Land – not to mention the ghastly Morisset on Norfolk Island – convicts sometimes faced a reign of terror, including chain gangs and places of special punishment. Rules for assigned prisoners became harsher. Yet many convicts could still negotiate wages or other benefits. The 300–400 convicts assigned to the Australian Agricultural Company in the 1830s were allowed to do extra work in exchange for rations, and there's evidence that convict mechanics and domestic servants received wages in the late 1830s. Even Governor Arthur's servants seem to have earned wages.[3]

It couldn't really be otherwise in colonies where labour was scarce. Although there was an adequate supply of governesses and domestic servants, there was considerable demand for farm servants, washerwomen, needlewomen and nursery maids. That caused endless headaches for a ruling class confronting an unruly working population. This situation, Elizabeth Macarthur complained, was both:

> a social evil, because it creates the greatest competition amongst employers for the services of labourers; and a political evil, because such a state of things tends to promote a democracy.[4]

In the 1820s, government immigration policies actually made labour scarcer by encouraging the arrival of people with capital and because 'nearly all the regulations...discriminated against the poorer immigrants.'[5] Bigge thought that assigned convicts would meet the labour needs of the affluent arrivals; but, by 1825, there were over 1,600 unfulfilled applications for convict labourers. Belatedly, after 1831, the authorities set about subsidising worker immigrants. Between 1832 and 1851, over 93,000 assisted migrants came to NSW, compared with 31,000 who came unassisted. But labour shortages continued, and the end of transportation in 1840 tightened the labour market even more.

The early decades of the 19th century saw 'free' labour start to replace convict labour. The difference was subtle. The two groups:

> were employed in the same occupations and on the same farms and stations. They often lived in the same huts and houses and in rural areas they generally received the same rations.

Living conditions were pretty hard for both, especially in the bush.[6] A mechanic, writing in 1852, recalled how convict exploitation shaped the employers' attitudes to free labour:

> Is not the free labourer here for our convenience – as a substitute for convicts who can no longer be found in sufficient numbers to supply us? What more profit is one to us than the other? Why should we treat one better than the other? Such is positively the feeling.[7]

While convicts achieved elements of freedom, the liberties of 'free' labour were circumscribed. Under the NSW Masters and Servants legislation, domestics entering contracts placed themselves under the employer's control 24 hours a day. Special laws governed friendly societies, vagrancy, hawkers and peddlers, Sunday observance, public entertainments, party processions and the behaviour of servants, apprentices and seamen. The criminal code was mainly devoted to punishing delinquency, securing property and safeguarding wealth. Moreover, additional laws to aid in capturing escaped convicts and bushrangers were frequently used to harass working people, while magistrates were hardly neutral. 'It should not be forgotten,' said Governor Gipps himself of the Masters and Servants laws, 'that the administration of the Act will be in the hands of the masters.'[8]

Industrial legislation partly derived from the laws used to control convicts. It differed from British labour law in a number of ways, reflecting the importance of rural industries and the high degree of state intervention. The colonial bourgeoisie needed its state to suppress Aboriginal and Torres Strait Islander people's resistance, provide extensive infrastructure, facilitate supply of both convict and free labour – and also discipline that labour. The need for discipline was greatest in the recurrent periods of acute labour shortage. The law condemned 'absconding' and restricted worker mobility generally. Many such measures were designed with an eye to conditions in the bush and aboard ships, where desertion was a chronic problem. Consequently, they were less effective against urban trade unions.

There were stiff curbs on domestic servants, because colonial domestics could be remarkably rebellious – especially if their labour was in short supply. In May 1845, the colonial press reported on the 'combination which at present exists amongst the female servants of Melbourne'. Some 20 domestics had applied to the magistrate for summonses against employers for non-payment of wages. The 'moment mistresses expressed dissatisfaction at finding work unperformed', the servants had 'left them and told them to do their work themselves.' When their employers withheld back pay, the magistrate reluctantly found for the domestics. The only way to contain the militancy was to import 50 or more 'respectable females' from Van Diemen's Land.[9]

TRADE UNIONISM

Worker resistance in the backblocks was likely to take on individual and sometimes anarchic forms. Stable working-class organisation could emerge more readily in the urban centres and on ships (which periodically came into port); not that there was a shortage of anarchic behaviour in the Sydney slums. The lower classes, who sustained about 800 licensed and unlicensed drinking establishments in a city of 20,000, drank partly as a form of social rebellion. The elite recognised and resented this fact. The *Sydney Morning Herald* complained in 1837 that, on one Sunday afternoon, 'a person could not turn a corner without running against a drunken beast'.[10]

But attempts at trade unionism also began early. The first recorded 'combination' of workers was in 1795, among reapers harvesting wheat. In 1806, four seamen were flogged around Sydney Cove for planning a 'mutiny'. In 1819, James Straiter:

> tried to organise a combination among the convict-shepherds bonded to Hannibal Macarthur to secure higher pay during the lambing-period. Straiter drew upon himself a penalty of 800 lashes and surviving them, made a marvellous recovery, but was punished further by transportation from Windsor to Port Macquarie.[11]

Waterside workers held protests over wages in the early 1820s, and a coopers' strike in 1824 spread to several other groups of employees.

The height of this early, semi-spontaneous round of class struggle was the 'currency' strike of 1829. Crisis had descended on the colony's jumbled money system when a sudden inflow of Spanish dollars caused confusion about the value of different currencies. With the local currency's value in doubt, the skilled workers of Sydney demanded payment in sterling, knowing that this implied a rise in real wages. The mechanics seeking to achieve that were simply attempting, like every other section of society, to turn the crisis to their own advantage; but the upper classes saw such self-assertion by the workers as a threat.

In 'a new and startling note', complained the conservative *Sydney Gazette*, 'labourers in many instances have combined to resist the commutation of wages.' The typographers of the rival

Australian newspaper led the movement, demanding £1 sterling in lieu of each 17 shillings 4 pence or £1 currency. The paper did not appear on Monday 30 November. Two days later, it consisted only of a sheet of advertisements and an explanation. 'The police were appealed to,' according to pioneering historian Leila Thomas, 'but with little success, their sympathies probably being with the strikers.' Although the *Australian's* editor vowed to refuse the pay increase out of a 'sense of justice to the Public in general and to employers of workmen in particular', lest it set a precedent for other enterprises, the typographers appear to have won a pay rise. In early December, a meeting of journeymen carpenters held a few miles from Sydney decided on an indefinite strike. Further, the crew of a whaler refused to sign the ship's articles until their demands were met. Other trades may well have been involved, 'for the public excitement seems to indicate a more or less general movement.' The agitation did not subside until the government intervened on 24 December to peg currency values.[12]

Although attempts were made to establish a Shipwrights' Society in 1829, the currency agitation did not give rise to stable union organisation. Unions did not begin to cohere until around 1833. Undoubtedly, the arrival of British immigrants with experience in unions and the Chartist movement assisted their formation. In the following years, up to the start of the 1850s, about 20 trade societies arose in Sydney to represent the 'operatives' of the town. With the settlement of other colonies, union organisation emerged fairly quickly in other parts of the continent; a dozen or so were reported in Port Phillip (Melbourne), where the carpenters and the bakers went on strike in 1840. The latter 'marched through the streets of the town, dodging stumps not yet removed by any Town Council' and burnt an effigy of the boss.[13] Twenty-three attempts to form unions are recorded in Van Diemen's Land (Tasmania) in the same years and 14 attempts in South Australia. Even the tiny settlement in Western Australia experienced union activity.

Most strikes between 1815 and 1859 actually involved unskilled workers rather than skilled operatives.[14] However, it was the latter who were better placed to form unions. They often began with friendly or benefit societies. This was partly out of a genuine need to provide health, unemployment and funeral assistance to members, and partly because the humanitarian rubric made it easier to avoid repression. The early unions also commonly sought to establish 'Houses of Call' – union hiring halls. They were invariably motivated by a desire to establish common rates of pay in their trades and to secure control of entry. Knowing that employers would seek to keep the labour market well supplied and highly competitive, they sought ways to limit competition.

The Cabinet Makers' Society, formed in Sydney in 1833, aimed to help its members 'insure their tools from loss by fire, and assist the widow and orphan in distress,' but also to secure piece rates at London levels. Other early unions included the Coachmakers, Seamen, Engineers, Cordwainers and the Boot and Shoemakers.

> But the strongest of all these early societies was formed when the Typographers established a fighting union, always remarkable for its aggressive spirit. It has a definite nine years' history, until June '44 at least.[15]

The early unions were generally quite craft-conscious and might not see the master as an adversary. If conflict did arise, they might not see it in class terms. Frequent reference to the 'working classes' in the plural indicated a limited class consciousness, while the slogan 'United to relieve, not combined to injure' signalled a defensive orientation. Strikes seem to have been rare in the 1830s, although the Boot and Shoemakers of Sydney struck for an advance in pay as early as 1831. But the caution was not just a matter of philosophy; it also reflected material conditions. Not only were the workers fragmented and isolated in small shops, where they were likely to feel a sense of responsibility for the survival of the business; they were also continually diluted by immigration.

Convict labour represented another threat. Bursts of prosperity in the 1830s allowed groups of workers to force wages up, but this was usually achieved through pressure short of strike action. The one recorded case of a fight for shorter working hours concerns the Assistant Drapers in Sydney, whose public agitation secured a reduction of hours from 14 to 12 for a year or so in the mid-1840s.

Not all skilled workers joined the unions, but even non-members would generally look to them for leadership in times of political agitation. Only 30 members attended the Compositors' first anniversary celebration in 1836, but this represented a majority of the estimated 48 journeymen in the colony. At the end of 1840, there were perhaps 300 unionists in Sydney; however, they were capable of calling meetings of 3,000–5,000. As a rule, the unions avoided long strikes, preferring short actions that could be repeated as pressure tactics until a compromise was reached. Still, there were some major battles.

The Compositors were one of the most confident unions in Sydney in the 1830s. Although they accepted a benefit society role, their constitution declared forthrightly that 'the chief aim of this union is the protection of labour'. The militant stance probably reflected the influence of 'red-hot radical' Peter Tyler, reputedly a Chartist and a 'mop' (a drunk). Under his leadership, the compositors struck successfully for a pay rise of five shillings in 1837 or 1838. But, at the end of the decade, they came under pressure from increased immigration, which the employers had actively promoted. In 1840, after the *Sydney Morning Herald* began taking on apprentices to dilute union strength, the compositors met and called for a set ratio of apprentices to journeymen. When the employers refused, the *Herald*'s compositors struck, whereupon the government provided convict labour to break the strike. Two compositors from the *Gazette* who got involved in the dispute were sentenced to two months' hard labour for leaving work without permission, and another who claimed sore eyes as a reason for missing work got 14 days.[16]

BURRA BURRA COPPER MINE, SOUTH AUSTRALIA

The 1841 recession hit hard. Assisted migrants, male and female, arrived to find that they had little hope of a job. The unions were obliged to fight several defensive struggles. In 1841, we find the bakers striking because one employer wanted to reduce wages, while another wanted to lay off workers and make the remaining employees do all the work. They won the first dispute, but lost the second when the government provided convict labour. Also in 1841, the Sydney bootmakers struck for a month but were defeated.

The level of industrial militancy tended to vary with the economic cycle. There were nine strikes in NSW in 1840 at the peak of prosperity, falling to four in 1841 as recession arrived. There were only two in the following three years; then the economic recovery years of 1845 and 1846 saw nine each. South Australia presented a similar picture, with strike activity peaking in 1839–1840 and again in 1846–47; the unions' main objectives were to standardise or improve wages. The onset of recession in South Australia in 1847, however, was followed by a major defensive struggle, ending in defeat, at the mining centre of Burra Burra (now Burra). It appears that union militancy followed the pattern we know from the later labour movement, with strikes generally more common when economic conditions raised workers' confidence, but some defensive struggles occurring during times of economic slump.[17]

The Burra Burra dispute was probably the largest strike in Australia before the gold rushes. This was a fabulously successful mine for the owners, whose shares had risen in value from £5 to £300 in 15 months; they had pocketed gigantic dividends. In August 1848, a dispute broke out over the terms of payment for a section of the work force, the 'tributers', who were on what amounted to individual contracts. The tributers temporarily occupied the mine and soon won the backing of other mine workers:

> Two men who went to work after these decisions were tied back to back and carried by the strikers on a hand barrow round the town and mine, followed by a crowd of several hundreds.[18]

Within days, a Friendly Society formed, with 343 members. The tributers won their demands. But the conflict revived a few days later, escalating to include all miners and even ore carriers, when management – presumably encouraged by the recession in the wider economy – imposed a general cut in wage and carriage rates. The mine workers waged a series of strikes but had to concede defeat when the ore carriers returned to work after three months. Although the owners had the benefit of large stockpiles, they were vulnerable because of financial mismanagement, and the strikers' defeat was by no means inevitable.[19]

The two groups of workers who engaged most frequently in collective struggle were whalers and merchant seamen. The close confinement in which they lived and worked fostered the growth of collective awareness and solidarity. This made it possible to challenge the employer, despite the draconian punishments to which they were usually liable. They enjoyed considerable public sympathy. In addition to frequent desertion, there were numerous cases of collective disobedience or refusal to work – in effect, strikes, although the term was seldom used. In the period 1829 to 1850, the Tasmanian press reported 20 such events.

So far, I've generalised about conditions Australia-wide. Let's consider the most important aspect of unevenness, that between Tasmania and South Australia. South Australia, settled under the Wakefield principles, was the colony where workers were most explicitly denied any hope of access to land; they were, therefore, most likely to look to industrial organisation to better their lot. At the same time, it was free of the convict labour that put such pressure on unions elsewhere. Prior to 1840, the market for skilled labour was tight, and wages were high – although they fell sharply in the recession of the early 1840s and didn't fully recover even when the economy turned up. In contrast, Tasmania was dominated by its role as a prison settlement. Free, skilled labour was perpetually on the defensive (except for seamen and whalers, whose occupations were excluded from convict assignment).

Consequently, there were only four strikes in Tasmania in the years before 1850, compared with 25 or more in South Australia. When skilled workers did strike, it was a defensive reaction to wage cuts; by and large, the Tasmanian societies devoted themselves to a political agitation against convictism:

[A] cluster of petitions in the period 1834–1839 reflected an intense effort by journeymen tailors, coopers, cordwainers and others to fight off the impact of convict assignment upon their wages and job prospects.[20]

The agitation was largely carried by individual trades; it did culminate in the formation of a 'Trades Union' (i.e., an organisation representing all crafts), but this was short lived. After assignment was abolished in 1843, the issue didn't go away. Rather, there was a shift to more political agitation against other aspects of the convict system.

We can see the dire effect of convictism on Tasmanian workers' industrial position by looking at pay. When Governor Arthur arrived on the island in 1824, wage levels were comparable with those in NSW. By the late 1840s, after Arthur and his successors had turned the island into a semi-Gulag, wages had fallen to around two-thirds of NSW levels.[21]

Because class divisions in a town like Sydney were so blurred, and the unions so new, the societies were not always clear about their role as independent organisations confronting the employer. 'Without union,' wrote Peter Tyler of the Compositors, 'we are completely at the mercy of our employers'. The Painters also saw a conflict with the masters, because the latter 'look for large profits and will not allow the workmen to do the work good or substantial'. On the other hand, the Engineers sought to advance 'the interests of the employer and the employed'. One unionist saw the formation of a House of Call as intended:

> not for the masters to give laws to their workmen nor for
> the workmen to give laws to their masters...but merely
> to confer a boon upon the employer and upon those to
> be employed.[22]

Workers were influenced by British theories, including political radicals ranging from Bentham to Robert Owen, the dominant ideas of contemporary political economy and various

THE PRISON STATE – HOBART

strands of Chartism. Chartists were leaders in the trade unions and in early colonial politics.

British radicalism had a strong democratic content, but its main representatives offered little to address the *specific* concerns of workers. From mainstream political economy, meanwhile, trade unionists got a concept of wages that pushed them in the direction of compromise and collaboration with their employers. The Melbourne operative sawyers might announce their unwillingness 'to become the dupes and slaves of those who think to monopolise our labour,' but such attitudes were usually based on an assumption that some mutually satisfactory arrangement was possible. 'We may see how very intimately

CHAIN GANG.

the two classes are bound together,' argued the pro-union *Star and Workingman's Guardian* in 1844:

> one cannot prosper without the other, for should the labourer demand wages above the intrinsic value of work done, the result is the destruction of the source from whence the labour is derived; whereas on the other hand, should the employer not pay the fair value for the labour done, he finds his loss by the decreased demand and diminished value of the commodity upon which that labour has been expended.[23]

Chartism had a more revolutionary flavour. But, translated into the Australian context, it still did not go beyond a radical democracy ultimately compatible with the existing social order. One strand emphasised education of the working class; a second emphasised trade union organisation and demands; a third looked to the establishment of cooperative ventures, either in the cities or on the land. There was agreement on the Charter itself, with its demand for universal suffrage and other democratic reforms. Ultimately, however, universal suffrage was to prove quite compatible with capitalism.

The bourgeoisie of the time were similarly ambiguous in their attitudes to the workers' organisations. At times, there was acute hostility. The *Port Phillip Patriot* growled in 1842:

> a dangerous feeling has of late evinced itself among a number of employed labourers who are daily to be seen idling at the door of the Registry Office, and who appear to have combined in order to extort a rate of wages preposterously high.

The paper quoted one Major St John as proposing, in his role as a magistrate, to commit them as rogues and vagabonds. Similarly, we have the pro-government *Sydney Gazette's* grumpy response to a newspaper strike:

> We trust the Chartist leader of the Sydney compositors and one or two more whom we could name may yet enjoy the blessing of a chain gang.[24]

Yet, even a wealthy landowner like W. C. Wentworth could, and did, rub shoulders with workers and pro-union middle-class radicals in a political movement when it suited him. Various currents in the bourgeoisie sought to mobilise the workers for their own ends – including rural interests, although it was the urban bourgeois radicals who were most successful.

Sydney workers first took an interest in politics because they faced unemployment. Large numbers of tradesmen had come out on assisted passage to work on construction of J. D. Lang's

Australian College. When college construction stopped in 1832, they were thrown out of work; then, in 1833, sizeable numbers of additional migrants arrived. The earlier arrivals' response displayed an irony to be repeated often in Australian history: the mechanics established a 'Society of Emigrant Mechanics' to seek cuts in migration! One tactic adopted, also to be used in subsequent crises, was the dispatch of 'authentic information' about conditions in Sydney to discourage prospective migrants. In addition, 'much excitement was caused' by a proposal to restrict convict labour, although this did not succeed.[25] The mechanics weren't hostile to the 'government men'; they simply saw competition from convict labour as a threat to their conditions.

In the end, the Emigrant Mechanics decided against political agitation, moving instead towards a broad cooperative welfare organisation. Initial proposals for a 'Trades Union Society' with a campaigning newspaper gave way to the Australian Union Benefit Society (AUBS), which was to confine itself to 'the relief of the working classes in New South Wales in the times of sickness, and other pecuniary distresses.' The AUBS survived well into the 20th century but always played a conservative role.[26]

The first major political movement in NSW was the Patriotic Association, formed in the mid-1830s to campaign for representative government. A large public meeting in January 1833 launched the campaign. In June 1835, further meetings approved proposals from W. C. Wentworth for a Directing Committee to take the lead. When Wentworth proposed that the committee consist of all persons who subscribed £5, the spectre of class raised its head: Wentworth's proposal would freeze out the workers, most of whom would be scratching to find £1. Richard Hipkiss, a leader of the middle-class radicals aligned with the unions, led an unsuccessful fight for a lower entry fee, and the 'trade union party' continued to argue for democratisation, both of the movement itself and of the proposed government structures. Wentworth was eventually forced to make concessions on the latter. In addition, the radicals argued in favour of land grants to small farmers, as opposed to open slather for the squatters; this was a first airing of the land issue.

The unions initially relied on Hipkiss and a range of other middle-class radicals to represent their interests within political movements. The key figures included William Duncan, Nathaniel Lipscombe, David Taylor, James McEachern, J. Bibb, W. Edwards, Henry Macdermott and Nathaniael Lipscomb Kentish; they formed an identifiable layer and were prominent in a series of organisations and movements. 'From the Committee of Emigrant Mechanics to the Mechanics' Institute they then proceeded through the AUBS to the Patriotic Association and wider political agitation.'[27] None was a former convict, and all seem to have been upwardly mobile, which perhaps helps to explain the rightward political evolution of their careers.

By 1839, Macdermott was a leading Sydney merchant and major employer. In the same year, Hipkiss, previously Wentworth's opponent, was lining up with him to support continued transportation; Kentish, an advocate of cooperation and foe of convictism, had also moved to a pro-transportation stance by the late 1830s. But it is equally likely that some of their original radical postures were opportunist. Duncan later wrote: 'Whoever would lead the people of NSW must follow them in the first place'.[28]

By the late 1830s, therefore, the workers had grounds to be disillusioned with their supposed representatives. In 1838, the unions began electing their own delegates to participate in public discussions. These delegates did not attend simply as individuals, nor yet merely as representatives of their crafts: they caucused periodically as a group, signalling an advance from craft consciousness to a wider class loyalty. Unfortunately, the advance was not sustained beyond the early 1840s; but, in the meantime, the workers did make some impact on colonial politics.

The defeat of Gipps' 1839 Corporation Bill limiting the political rights of emancipists was partly due to working-class agitation, prompting Duncan to declare that they were becoming 'much more independent in their habits than their predecessors, the assigned convicts, had been'. A year later, there was considerable worker opposition to a new Masters and Servants Bill. Duncan inaugurated the opposition campaign with a series of newspaper articles written in plain language for a worker readership. The operatives called a public meeting on 30 September which endorsed a petition; by 11 am the next day, they had collected 3,000 signatures. The government was sufficiently impressed to water down the Act, and a stiffer one was not passed until 1845. It was the first occasion, wrote Duncan, when 'the real colonists, the real producers of wealth first informed the drones of the hive... that the latter *were* but drones'.[29]

In September 1842, the squatters began agitating for the systematic introduction of Asian labour. This followed the recession, in which they had responded to lower wool prices by cutting wages. In union eyes, one threat had followed another, and the trades called a mass meeting on 16 January. Some of the agitation was undeniably racist: a mass petition warned of the 'vices particular to the Natives of India' which would hinder 'the growth of virtue and morality amongst us'.[30] It was the start of a long and unfortunate tradition in the Australian labour movement. On the other hand, the meeting, which showed signs of Chartist influence, also had a class dimension: one of the speakers, G. L. Nichols, argued that 'the present question was one between the whole body of the working class and the great flockmasters of the colony'.[31]

The radical and working-class movements in Sydney saw the 'flockmasters' as the main enemy – partly because class differences in the town were comparatively blurred, and partly because workers made miserable by capitalist industry yearned for land of their own. The people as a whole, and especially the common people, believed that they had some inherent right to the land. Such ideas had an attraction even for those skilled workers who had no intention of heading for the back blocks, because an exodus of their fellow tradespeople from the cities would have drained the market of potential competitors. This would assist them in their own desire to become affluent master craftsmen. What united thousands was the cry of independence from the oppression of wage labour.

Mid-year, a campaign against convictism saw union delegates call a mass meeting at the racecourse. Some 3,000 attended. The crowd wanted to march on Government House, but Duncan and Macdermott restrained them. Instead, the meeting selected a group to go door-to-door, gathering information about distress in the town. The facts they gathered put the authorities under pressure and extracted some relief measures, but government rejection of the workers' petition fuelled proposals for a new political party. The Mutual Protection Association (MPA), established on 29 August, grew quickly from 18 members to several hundred. It established its own paper, *The Guardian*, assisted by union funds, and was able to get six candidates, clearly identified as representing working-class interests, elected to the city council in 1844.

The MPA's objectives included an 'endeavour to impress upon all the community the need of cooperation', a focus on economic distress, a pledge to 'resist class legislation' and 'watch over the interests of the working class' and also a commitment to 'foster and encourage colonial produce and manufacture'.[32] The group's platform thus contained elements of class struggle, but equally raised proposals that would align workers with employers. However, the formulations were all fairly vague: the workers hadn't even arrived at the demand that governments should intervene to regulate wages and working conditions.

CONTRADICTIONS

The MPA marked a high point of the movement. Yet, because of its political contradictions, it also heralded a collapse. Despite looking for an explicitly political expression, the workers didn't

FRONT PAGE OF THE FIRST ISSUE OF *THE GUARDIAN* 16 MARCH 1844

take the lead themselves. Perhaps their confidence had been undermined by the economic recession; it was at this point that they abandoned their system of directly elected delegates. The MPA included non-unionists and members of the middle class alongside the union members, and the leading figures were again drawn from the middle class.

The MPA seems to have been very active in the political life of the colony, generating innumerable meetings, petitions, deputations and inquiries and apparently persuading the Legislative Council to appoint a Commission on Distressed Labourers in 1844. Among the petitions was one 'signed by upwards of 1,000 females, the wives and dependents of the working classes', insisting that, because the men's unemployment and reduced wages forced them to take in washing, 'that the washing establishments at the female factory, at Parramatta, might be discontinued.' The Colonial Secretary apparently expressed agreement, although nothing was done.[33]

By April 1844, the Association began to split. The original *Guardian* editor, James McEachern, who had flailed the 'colonial autocracy', was replaced by Benjamin Sutherland, who set a tone more sympathetic to the squatters. Workers were frustrated by Gipps' rejection of their demands and the indifference of the British authorities (the Colonial Secretary responded to complaints that wages for relief work were inadequate by retorting that they were only meant to prevent starvation). A section of the MPA was attracted to the squatters' cause because they, too, were in conflict with the governor. It appears that at least some of the workers in the MPA favoured the pro-squatter line, while many of the middle-class radicals bitterly opposed it.

The Guardian argued that the government had ignored appeals to provide work for the unemployed, so there was no solution for unemployment but to revive the economy. It thought that Gipps' restrictions on the squatters would impede that revival. We see in this line of argument the dilemma of a movement trapped between futile appeals to an autocratic governor and falling in behind the reactionary landowners. The silver lining was that *The Guardian* was at least challenging the dominant notion that the landowners were the only enemy. Without a new class analysis to fill the void, however, the result was confusion. By the end of the year, the MPA was in terminal decline. Another attempt to form an 'association of the working class' in 1849 met with little success.

Events in Tasmania and South Australia offer some useful comparisons with those in NSW. In these colonies, as in Western Australia, workers were less likely than in Sydney to have realistic hopes of rising into the middle and upper classes. For South Australia, the schemer Edward Gibbon Wakefield dictated that land be sold at a premium to affluent settlers, with the proceeds going to import labour for their use. The high land prices were designed to keep workers from escaping the labour market. In Tasmania, most of the land had been locked up by the end of the 1820s, and wages were too low for most workers to get ahead:

> In sum, these were colonies where opportunities for workers to become landowners, merchants or other employers were

extremely limited and few could even aspire to the status of self employment.[34]

While there were important union-based political mobilisations in both colonies, the issues were very different. In Tasmania, where convict competition undermined industrial organisation, opposition to it became a major political rallying point for labour. There is some evidence of worker agitation on the issue in the 1820s, but the first significant mobilisation coincided with an initial phase of union organisation in the mid-1830s. In August 1844, at a time of widespread unemployment, the skilled trades developed a major campaign, presenting elaborate petitions to the governor and the British Government calling for an end to the probation passholder system, under which convicts in the colony worked for wages under highly restrictive conditions. The agitation 'gave rise to an identifiable worker leadership which was careful to avoid a divisive split between free emigrants and ex-convicts'.[35] A body called the Committee of Free Operatives arose in Hobart and remained active for well over a year.

In 1847, and again in 1851, labour protests against convictism revived in both Hobart and Launceston. The Operatives Committee revived as the Committee of the Free Working Classes, then evolved into the Hobart Town Trades Union, which survived until 1852. These bodies represented most trades as well as labourers and other workers. When petitions proved ineffectual, the activists organised contingents to public meetings. In 1851, the Trades Union was influential in securing the election of at least one anti-transportationist to the Legislative Council. The establishment of the Launceston Working Men's Association in 1849 was also associated with the anti-transportation cause. The workers' organisations collaborated with employers and other groups who opposed convictism, but the Hobart Town Trades Union was also to show, in its agitation against the amended *Master and Servant Act* in 1855–56, that it was an independent force.

VICTORIAN PLASTERERS' UNION BANNER, 1856

In South Australia, among a diversity of issues, a major focus of political agitation was the slump of the early 1840s. It hit South Australia particularly hard. Under Governor Gawler, the colony had expanded rapidly, partly because of generous levels of public expenditure. Then, incompetent management of public finance led to a crisis of confidence in 1840, triggering Gawler's replacement by Grey, whose draconian austerity policies provoked unrest.

In November 1841, nearly one-sixth of the total population depended on some form of government relief. When Grey cut relief payments, eliminating them altogether for those refusing to go and work in the bush, unionists formed a Working Men's Association to demand a change of policy. This campaign was unsuccessful, although a group of worker agitators almost captured a public meeting called by the Chamber of Commerce to consider distress in the community. In 1847, meetings in the working-class suburb of Hindmarsh condemned the government's new Master and Servant Bill, and rural workers and miners protested. 'All three groups sent strongly worded memorials to the Governor pledging that they would have no truck with the new law',[36] and the agitation secured some modification of the Bill.

Finally, with self-government on the agenda, the workers of Hindmarsh set up an Elective Franchise Association in 1850, led by militant bootmaker George Wells. It called for universal suffrage, vote by ballot, annual elections, no religious endowment by the state and abolition of British control of the land fund. The Complete Suffrage League later joined this group; the two organisations then merged to form the South Australian Political Association, which 'eschewed seeking middle-class support for its objects'.[37]

Probably because they had less hope of achieving economic independence, Tasmanian and South Australian workers seem to have been more consistently class conscious than their contemporaries in NSW. In South Australia, there was even talk of socialism. George Wells declared to one newspaper editor:

> You speak of working men as degraded beings and
> willingly enter the lists on behalf of employers. The reason
> why, I suppose, is because they belong to your class.

The view that workers' labour was the source of all wealth was widespread, and the chairman of one trade society was prepared to argue that the interests of masters and journeymen were counterposed; combination, he added, was 'socialism itself and therefore radically good'.[38]

However, these were minority views. The early workers' movement never challenged the social order as a whole. Trade unionists claimed the 'rights of Englishmen' or perhaps something a bit better: the hope that the evils of the old world could be avoided in the new. The slogan 'United to Protect, Not Combined to Injure' was used not only to deflect criticism, but also to hold out an olive branch. Yet, the unions' very existence signalled the emerging division of White Australia into the two great social classes, capital and labour, whose struggle has shaped its subsequent history.

2.
A POWER IN THE LAND

AUSTRALIAN UNIONS, 1855–1890

It was a time of hope. While most unions had melted away among the gold rushes of the early 1850s, workers rebuilt them from scratch by the middle of the decade. The subsequent 45 years saw three peak periods of strike activity, mostly associated with the struggle for the eight-hour day. The first, and most successful, was centred in Victoria shortly after the gold rushes. The second and third, in NSW during the early 1860s and early 1870s, featured metal workers and coal miners.

Some New Zealand building trades had achieved an eight-hour day in the 1840s, and Sydney stonemasons were the first to do so in Australia. It was Victoria, however, that experienced a great campaign extending beyond the purely industrial sphere. The issue preoccupied far more people than the minority of workers who actually won the shorter hours; it was a defining, long-term aspiration for the labour movement as a whole. 'By 1881, fifty-six of the seventy-six unions in Melbourne had their origins in demands for an eight hour day.'[1]

Although the Victorian economy was still fragile, wages were significantly higher than in Britain, allowing some skilled workers to focus more on improving working conditions. They aspired to more leisure time as part of a climate of social optimism that was strongest in the middle classes but also vibrant among the skilled trades. Cultural life flowered. Mechanics' Institutes sought to uplift the labouring classes through libraries, lectures and musical performances. The future would surely be more edifying still, and workers wanted to share in the improvements; indeed, they *needed* to share in them, because working men would soon be called upon to vote. To prepare themselves, they needed 'the sacred gift of time'.[2]

Shop Assistants had been agitating for early closing since 1846. The most pious elements in the community endorsed the call for shorter hours, hoping that greater leisure would encourage church attendance. Others believed that the hot Australian sun made longer hours intolerable for delicate Europeans. This was, in other words, a very respectable demand; small wonder that the conservative Mayor of Melbourne became president of the Early Closing Association. By mid-1856, shops were closing earlier throughout the colony, adding further momentum to union demands for shorter working hours.

When the Operative Masons approached the Builders' Association on 5 March, the bosses were generally agreeable. Other building trades followed rapidly, and 21 April was set as the day to introduce the new arrangements. A public meeting of various trades and occupations was held on 11 April:

> The Queen's Theatre was packed; the Mayor assumed the chair. Leading radicals took the unions' part, stressing the need for amicable relations between employers and employees, as well as the case for shorter hours. It was claimed 'that the old idea that prevailed at home that one class was born to labour and another to direct that labour ought not to find a place here.'[3]

8 HOUR DAY DEMONSTRATION ADELAIDE, 1885

Two major employers resisted. To bring them to heel, Melbourne's construction workers marched from the university, pulling unionists off building sites as they went. The concluding rally at Eastern Hill (East Melbourne) endorsed a strike. One of the recalcitrant bosses caved in that evening, and government pressure ensured that the other complied the following day.

The agitation spread. An Eight Hours League mobilised the general citizenry. Painters and paperhangers, plumbers and cabinet makers, all trades close to the building industry, gained the eight-hour day with no reduction in pay. Other trades found it much harder. Construction faced no foreign competition, so it could sustain a considerably higher cost structure than in Britain. Many other industries, however, were more exposed. In the 1850s, the building industry was still full of small subcontractors who had only recently been employees themselves and thought that they might soon be again. To them, the eight-hour day seemed to be in the interests of the industry as a whole. Bosses in other sectors were less likely to think this way.

Saddlers, harness and collar-makers, ironworkers and coachmakers all had to accept lower pay to get shorter hours, the coachmakers doing so after a prolonged strike in 1856. The following year, bakers and butchers, who worked in small establishments alongside the employer, did win shorter hours without pay cuts. Outside Melbourne, however, the shorter hours movement did not extend much beyond the building trades.

Railway construction from Melbourne to Bendigo and Geelong to Ballarat began in 1858. This eased the unemployment problem. Wages rose, and the unions demanded a shorter working day on the construction projects. Unfortunately, the work was so dispersed that employees couldn't organise to get full benefit from the economic conditions. Subcontracting arrangements undermined pay and conditions, and workers sometimes found it hard to collect wages. The employers tried to break the union by importing labour, firstly hiring 10 masons from South Australia to work a 10-hour day. When the new arrivals discovered what was afoot, they joined the strike. After the bosses had them arrested and charged, two radical barristers successfully defended them.

In November, the union, having learned that 200 German masons were on their way, managed to contact them on the ship and convince the majority not to scab. Most absconded to find jobs in the bush, although a few were forced to fulfil their contracts. Industrial conflict continued while they remained employed, 'but it remained a remarkable feature of the dispute that all attempts to set off "foreign" against British workmen were unsuccessful.'[4]

In Melbourne, a revived Eight Hours League held large public meetings in support of the strike. There was much discussion of tariff protection as a way to guarantee shorter wages and hours, so these public mobilisations fed into the protectionist movement.

Conditions for unions were generally less favourable in NSW. Apart from some of the building trades, unionists found it extremely hard to win the eight-hour day. The first major battle was the 1861 strike at P. N. Russell and Co., Sydney's main engineering works.

Labour relations here were poisonous. Workers reported that management underpaid them and hit them with blacklists as well as various petty tyrannies. When management demanded a 10 percent pay cut, 20 to 30 blacksmiths, fitters and turners struck; over the following two months, another 30 left the job. Within weeks, 300 tradespeople had affirmed their support for the strike, and £50 a week was coming in from as far away as Newcastle and Melbourne. Next, the company's moulders demanded the eight-hour day, joining the strike when management refused. The ironworkers then added this demand to their own claim. The engineers' union (ASE) helped the unskilled workers to form a separate association and join the struggle.

The wages issue now had second billing, with unions calling for an eight-hour day throughout the trade. Some smaller employers were sympathetic, but most waited to see the outcome at Russell. Management prosecuted two unionists on conspiracy charges. The trial ended in acquittal, but the legal costs drained the strike fund, and the company was recruiting scabs. Increasing numbers of strikers drifted into other jobs, off to the New Zealand goldfields or back to work.

The strike largely ended in failure, as did the push for shorter hours, although some moulders achieved an eight-hour day. Sections of the building trades were inspired to go out and get it as well. Perhaps the unions had made mistakes in tackling Russell at this stage and in linking the eight hours issue to the dispute. Although unemployment had fallen from a peak in 1860, economic conditions were still not favourable to the unions.

They weren't especially good in the coal fields, either. The coal mining industry had begun with convict labour under the Australian Agricultural Company (AAC). Until the 1870s, it was based overwhelmingly in the Hunter Valley. Under the impact of the gold rushes, coal prices and wages rose between 1851 and 1855, a period that saw three successful strikes. By 1855, gold production was falling, and the AAC imposed wage cuts. The miners struck, to no avail: with coal stockpiles high and demand falling, the strike front broke after two and a half months, militants were victimised, and management boasted that the 'incorrigible and turbulent hands had been got rid of'.[5]

However, the industry kept growing. Coal production grew fivefold between 1850 and 1860, owing to demand from the railways. By 1861, there were four major employers in the Newcastle area. Worker organisation revived to the point where, for the first time, miners set about uniting the various local lodges into a wider organisation. Up to 1,000 assembled in May to launch the Hunter River Coalminers' Protective Association, the Minmi lodge marching up behind a tricolour flag reading: 'United We Stand, Divided We Fall'.[6] It was a timely sentiment; by October, the Minmi lodge were on strike. The new Association organised a 500-strong demonstration and convinced non-unionists to stop work in their support.

The four main proprietors responded by joining forces against 'the unjust and exorbitant demands of the miners'[7] – giving 14 days' notice of a 20 percent pay cut and laying plans to import 400 strikebreakers from England. The unionists struck again, their wives and daughters fighting alongside them, as was already traditional in the coal fields:

> The miners' womenfolk followed sailors loading coal,
> with banging of tins and shouting... When police escorting
> the blacklegs tried to arrest the women the strikers took
> a hand and forced the police to retire. [A police constable
> said the women] were pulling his hair and whiskers...as

they could not work because of the women throwing coal at them the men went back to Newcastle.[8]

The bosses backed down temporarily but returned to the offensive a year later, led by AAC manager J. B. Winship. Winship's main tactic was to import unemployed miners from the now-depressed Victorian goldfields. Some of these were indeed desperate. 'In fact they are almost starving,' wrote a gleeful Winship, who took a direct hand in recruiting them.[9] Even so, many refused to scab. Though he recruited 300, he believed that he could have signed up 1,000 if news of the strike had not reached Victoria. Unionists won over probably half of these 300 on arrival by slipping them leaflets and inviting them to meetings at night.

Nevertheless, after seven months, the miners' resistance collapsed. Once again, unionism seemed to be thoroughly smashed. Coal production continued to rise throughout the decade, but always ahead of demand, ensuring cutthroat competition between the companies and weakening workers' bargaining position.

The union defeats of the 1860s in NSW owed much to a difficult economic climate, but this doesn't explain everything. Economic conditions were by no means ideal in the early 1870s, when organised labour did rather better. The defeats also resulted from unions' inexperience and inability to control the flow of labour. By the 1870s, the industrial movement had gained in both experience and organisation. A rise in the sheer numerical size of the work force, and consequently in union numbers, also brought the unions greater stability.

In 1871, NSW had a sharp recession. As it faded, real wages began to rise, and there were again signs of union revival. The Hunter River miners began rebuilding their regional organisation, waging 'a continuous struggle...to establish the authority of the association and police job conditions.'[10] In 1873, they demanded a 10-hour shift. The employers insisted on 11 hours, sacking those who refused. After a six-week lockout, stoning of scabs, several shots fired by police and the jailing of one woman for assaulting a constable, the two sides agreed to implement the 10-hour shift by 1874.

Unionism was also advancing in the iron trades, with the rise of organisations for plumbers, boilermakers, tinsmiths and moulders. This was part of a general trend symbolised by the 1871 formation of the Sydney Trades and Labour Council (TLC). Progress on the eight-hour day was slow at first, because of union disagreements over whether to accept a proportionate cut in pay. Some tradesmen accepted this, reckoning that a shortening of hours would tighten the labour market and push wages up again; but labourers, already on near-subsistence wages, had no patience with such theories. By 1873, only one major firm, the A.S.N. company, was working the shorter day.

Finally, the engineering unions put together a common set of demands, including the eight-hour day with two breaks. A few days later, Mort's Dock sacked several men, provoking a mass walkout. In negotiations, proprietor T. S. Mort apparently convinced the strikers that the dismissals were not industrial victimisation, then conceded the shorter day – but he demanded wage adjustments, only backing down after further strike action.

The other company to resist was that old union bogey, P. N. Russell and Co., which opposed the afternoon meal break. Although a short stoppage forced the company into line, the meal breaks issue quickly re-emerged throughout the trade. The two-break system meant that forges had to be relit and casting run-offs prepared anew, late in the day, for the last two hours. The proprietors claimed that this was uneconomical. They imposed roster changes, causing 2,000 unionists to stop work for two months.

The TLC was raising funds from its affiliates and from Melbourne, while the local companies were losing contracts to Victorian rivals. Still, the proprietors grimly held out. Union delegates proposed arbitration, as did the TLC; the employers said

WORKERS AT P. N. RUSSELL AND CO., SYDNEY, 1871

that a technologically unworkable system could not be arbitrated. The TLC organised 'monster meetings' to mobilise public support, while the press fulminated against the 'narrow, selfish and irrational views of a few' allegedly manipulating the strikers.[11]

As the public weighed up the opposing arguments, the ironmasters fretted that £50,000 worth of orders had been lost. Finally, they and the TLC settled on a 10-minute break. When union members rejected this offer:

> an emergency meeting of strikers was called on 2 March, at which the delegates were empowered to reach a settlement without reference back to the rank and file.

The meeting accepted a compromise involving two breaks in summer and one in winter. The employers also agreed not to alter rosters again without 'the concurrence of the majority of the mechanics in the shops'.[12]

At the end of the post-gold rush period, despite some cruel setbacks, the unions could congratulate themselves on winning gains and then defending and entrenching them. With success, however, came conservatising tendencies. The first signs of a top-down, bureaucratic leadership style had appeared in the metal trades dispute, when rank-and-file metal workers lost decision-making power after rejecting a strike settlement. Unions were also beginning to call for arbitration as an alternative to industrial struggle.

Even in the coal industry, with its turbulent history and militant traditions, there was a certain respect for the 'masters', expressed in invitations to attend union picnics (offers the proprietors generally ignored) and a certain notion of common interest. Union attempts to encourage cooperation among the employers to reduce competition reinforced the latter. Although the 1873 coal strike was very bitter, the miners still declared that they were 'following the example of the English miners, not the Communists of Paris.' The general agreement ending the strike provided for pegging wages to profits and the settling of disputes by arbitration, so that 'strikes and lock-outs would be a thing of the past.'[13] Vain hope!

A 'NEW UNIONISM'

Union actions were growing bigger. Where perhaps 300 masons had waged the biggest dispute in Victoria in the 1850s, more like 1,000 NSW coal miners had struck in 1861 and 2,000–3,000 in 1874. The number of striking NSW ironworkers was also larger in the 1870s than in the 1860s.[14] Further, new sectors were emerging; in transport, for example, carters and drivers unionised. Existing sectors were becoming more union conscious. In 1874, 12 Victorian metal miners' unions merged to form the Amalgamated Miners'

Association (AMA). Four years later, William Guthrie Spence organised the miners at Creswick.

Other new unions formed. Seafarers united in Melbourne and Sydney in the mid-1870s. This union set two historic precedents in 1878 – one baleful, another more encouraging. After the Australian Steam and Navigation Company moved to replace Australian crews with lower-paid Chinese crews, Australian seamen walked off ships in Sydney, Newcastle, Brisbane and ports further north. The dispute ended in a political victory for those opposed to Chinese labour.

Industrially, the victory was not terribly impressive. The union initially offered a no-strike agreement in exchange for sending the Chinese home; and the final settlement, reached with ample strike funds remaining, allowed scabs to remain employed while well over 100 unionists remained out of work. The successes owed as much to public opinion and government pressure on the company (because of the race issue) as to industrial action. However, the sheer fact of an inter-colonial strike by unskilled labour was significant.[15]

Over the 1880s, union membership reached 60,000. Unionism came to the railways and to the maritime and pastoral industries, drawing new layers of workers – many unskilled – into what has been called a 'new unionism'.

The term itself, drawn from British labour history, can be misleading. It has been taken to mean that organisation of the unskilled and semiskilled was a radical innovation, that the new unions were all committed to industrial unionism, and that they were more militant than traditional craft organisations. Strictly speaking, none of this is true. Mass organisation of unskilled and semiskilled workers in mines and on the waterfront existed well before the 1880s. On the other hand, the Australian Shearers' Union operated much like the craft unions, organising the elite of the pastoral work force, and it was by no means more militant than the stonemasons.[16]

SOUTH AUSTRALIAN SEAMEN'S UNION BANNER, 1880

Something new certainly happened in the 1880s, driven by changes in capitalist industry. Companies that had previously brought together concentrations of relatively expensive skilled labour now began replacing that labour with machinery. As industry became mechanised, the need to use capital equipment efficiently led to larger concentrations of unskilled and semi-skilled workers. Mechanisation also stimulated other industries by increasing the demand for raw materials, such as meat and sugar, and for expanded rail and sea transport. Here, too, large new workforces emerged. In enterprises where high numbers of poorly paid labourers all did the same work, common experiences bred solidarity, while unskilled workers' lack of individual bargaining power made the case for organisation and mass action more compelling.

The term 'unskilled' can also be misleading. Many workers with no formal craft status did have skills; what they lacked was a strategic monopoly in those skills. Women in the clothing trades were adept at sewing; but, because most other women could also sew, companies could easily replace them, putting them in a similar industrial position to the genuinely unskilled. But we'll use the term for want of a better one.

The majority of the unskilled were not unionised, and unskilled or semiskilled workers did not come to dominate the labour movement. On the contrary, delegates to the 1888 Intercolonial Trade Union Congress still lamented:

> tradesmen were united as a rule, and unionists were pretty well protected; but what was wanted was the organisation of unskilled labour, so that all might be protected.[17]

Even so, unionism had reached enough unskilled and semi-skilled workers to alter the industrial scene. Strikes became bigger and longer, providing practical experience of solidarity. Where workers formed a new union or won a strike, others followed their example.

Some unions also set about organising others. Seafarers and railway workers were always on the move, carrying ideas of unionism wherever they travelled. So were shearers. The westward expansion of the pastoral industry lengthened the shearing season and concentrated workers in larger gangs – conditions that fostered solidarity. In the cities, meanwhile, settled working-class suburbs grew up where residents could mobilise in support of union action, just like mining towns.

Numerical growth in union membership, alongside the merger of local organisations into intra- and inter-colonial unions, began to raise the conflict between employer and employee from a series of local episodes to an ongoing, continent-wide affair.

Unskilled and semiskilled workers, denied the modest element of individual self-sufficiency and control of the labour process enjoyed by craft labour, were more interested in ideas that the union movement should fight for control of the workplace, or that the state should intervene.[18]

We begin to see why so many embraced unionism (in Spence's words) 'as a religion',[19] why some capitalists felt so threatened by it, and why radical ideologies began to make themselves heard. It is not that unionism, let alone socialist politics, developed spontaneously. A small army of agitators moved amongst the workers, fighting to convince and organise them, with many heartbreaking failures amongst the successes; but capitalist development opened up the possibilities.

The manufacturing boom drew thousands of women into factory life and into outwork, especially in Victoria. Large numbers joined the garment trade. Some of this industry's features mirrored traditional domestic labour, and it offered the option of outwork; joining it didn't seem to be such a radical departure from the established female role. Soon, however, women's experience in industry began to challenge that role. In tailoring, especially, young females set out to acquire marketable skills and thereby achieve a certain independence, so that 'the tailoring factories seem to have attracted a more outspoken and independent type of woman.' In the late 1880s, the Chief Inspector of Factories complained that 'the factory work girl' was 'a very difficult person to deal with', apparently for the very reason that she was 'as a rule able to take care of herself'.[20]

Unfortunately, growth in the work force also put downward pressure on women's piece rates. With the number of clothing and textile factories in Victoria rising from around 70 to well over 200 in the decade ending 1881, intensified competition drove employers to cut costs. Local, sporadic strike action in the tailoring factories failed to prevent this, because the bosses easily found strike breakers. Ellen Cresswell, soon to be a leader of the Tailoresses' Association, was herself victimised after a strike in 1879.

These pay cuts reached a crisis point in 1882, when companies began making tailoresses do order work at the rates applied to ready-made garments. In December 1882, the workers struck, beginning at Beath, Schiess and Co. Hundreds of women came to the Trades Hall seeking help in forming a union. At a second meeting of 400–500, supported by another 500 sympathisers assembled outside the building, the Tailoresses' Association took shape. The strikers elected a committee to lead the struggle together with a group of Trades Hall officials. The first round of the campaign ended before Christmas, with the company agreeing to meet union demands if others did the same.

As with the eight-hour day campaigns, the new union enjoyed support from some employers and a wide cross-section of the community. Increasingly, the ideology of protectionism united the union movement with sections of capital. Not only did *The Age* newspaper back the strike, but Beath, Schiess and Co. were themselves not entirely opposed to it. Company manager J. R. Blencowe attended a meeting at Trades Hall, indicating that the firm would meet the demands as long as the whole industry was organised. He added:

> so far as Beath, Schiess and Co. were concerned, [they] did not care if the prices were increased by one hundred percent if all the other firms joined in the movement.[21]

Some other major employers apparently also hoped that it would prevent the smaller shops from undercutting them. Victoria's system of protective tariffs had allowed a variety of small operators to spring up, and those with fewer than 10 employees were exempt from the *Shops and Factories Act 1873*. If unions could enforce uniform rates throughout the industry, the big companies would benefit.

In the new year, the other bosses showed less enthusiasm for the union's claims. By mid-February, around 1,200 tailoresses were on strike. At the end of the month, most employers seem to have acquiesced, although picketing continued as late as April. Some accounts say that the union rates prevailed for a couple of years, but nine of the strikers later told the Shops Commission that:

> while the manufacturers had, at the time, agreed to pay the log, very few adhered to it for more than a few weeks after the return to work.[22]

It appears that companies got around the union by contracting work out.

During the 1880s, union membership declined from more than 2,000 in 1883 to 100 or so in 1890. The strike was, nonetheless, a landmark in raising public awareness about working conditions. It gave a huge boost to the anti-sweating campaign and also to the struggle for the eight-hour day. Of course, it is also important as the first major industrial struggle by women, making it the subject of considerable debate.

The example of solidarity between male and female trade unionists seems to rankle with some feminist historians. For example, Anne Summers suggests that the strike was motivated entirely by male tailors' selfish desire to avoid competition from cheaper, female labour.[23] Influenced by this argument, Ken Buckley and Ted Wheelwright similarly remark that such acts of solidarity were 'not always as altruistic as they seemed'.[24] However, such comments miss the point. No large body of people ever forgets about self-interest for long; the issue is how they pursue it. Rather than dividing along gender lines, the Victorian labour movement understood that it was in the interest of all workers to support the tailoresses. The triumph of solidarity in 1882–83 was important because it demonstrated a viable alternative to gender divisions in the working class.

Raelene Frances makes a more sophisticated argument. In her eyes, the unity, while a positive thing, came about partly because women were 'accustomed to the direction of men' and because these 'helpless girls', as *The Age* called them (but Frances seems to agree) needed help in a way male unionists did not – male unions being 'generally jealous of their own independence.'[25] Yet Frances herself reports elsewhere that the tailoresses had tried striking on their own and only approached Trades Hall after they failed. They didn't lack independent spirit; they just wished to learn from experience and benefit from solidarity. Frances notes that the strike set a precedent for other unions – in other words, the tailoresses were pioneers. A few years later, the Yarra River waterside workers were to learn many of the same lessons.

In any case, as Frances also reports, waging a strike helped women *break out* of conventional roles. They picketed outside factories, using 'violent language and threats' against scabs, and employers complained that they were 'very difficult to deal with', having 'no faith in what you say'.[26]

The following years saw a strike by male bootmakers. Theirs was a highly competitive trade whose bosses had a history of ruthless wage cuts, victimisation and child labour. The Operative Bootmakers' Union arose in 1879 and grew rapidly, claiming 1,000 members by 1882. Union secretary W. A. Trenwith was a former boxer who finished his career as a member of parliament; in the 1880s, he also proved a dynamic industrial organiser, producing posters identifying scabs by name and branding them as traitors. A series of strikes in 1883 compelled the employers to accept a union log of claims, and a board of conciliation formed with 14 representatives from each side.

This union had low fees, did not initially provide benefits, and in 1884 began admitting semiskilled workers. It was a good example of 'new unionism'. Late in the same year, the bosses locked the men out in a dispute over outwork, provoking a major industrial conflagration. The Victorian Trades Hall Council (THC) assumed leadership and raised over £9,000 in contributions and levies. There were brawls on picket lines, and strikers suffered hardship, although the greatest hardship confronted the 700 women and girls stood down with no strike pay.

Within three months, the bosses began to give way. In February 1885, they agreed to eliminate outwork except where special safeguards applied. On the other hand, the union gave away its right to enter workplaces. It was not a complete union victory, but the bootmakers' strike alarmed employer representatives, who thought that the owners were proving unable to match the solidarity of organised labour. A meeting of capitalists in early 1885 called for the formation of a militant bosses' organisation. Bruce Smith, who wrote at the time that bosses' and workers' interests were 'antagonistic', made the keynote speech at the Employers' Union's founding meeting; he later recalled being in a 'savage' frame of mind because of industrial unrest in the maritime industry.[27] Before the decade was out, this body had 500 member firms. Just as capitalism had given rise to a labour movement, now labour's struggles were stimulating more coherent organisation among the capitalists. Both began to take on continent-wide dimensions, beginning with the maritime industry.

'CAPITAL VERSUS LABOUR'

Victoria's waterfront unions first took root in the bayside communities of Sandridge (Port Melbourne) and Williamstown in the 1870s. The Yarra River wharves near central Melbourne remained unorganised until 1885, despite some local strikes. In 1884, the Yarra watersiders staged their first total walkout over hours, pay and hiring practices but found themselves at a disadvantage without stable organisation and solidarity from other unions. When the ship owners outraged wharfies by refusing to let them attend the Eight Hours anniversary march in 1885, Trades Hall representatives stepped in, and the Melbourne Wharf Labourers' Union was formed. The union served a log on the employers in September and had it refused. On 1 January 1886, around 900 workers shut down the Yarra shipping industry. During the 18-day stoppage, mass pickets effectively prevented deliveries, with Port Phillip stevedores refusing to work ships diverted from the Yarraside. Yardmen and draymen also struck, as did the wharf labourers of Geelong, who established a union of their own.

The Employers' Union declared it 'the bounden duty of every employer' to back the waterfront bosses, putting the screws on one company that had settled. Ship owners, aware of unemployment in other colonies, offered attractive pay to strikebreakers. Ninety-four unemployed men came from Adelaide, but unionists won them over. Attempts to secure 'volunteer' labour from Bendigo and even from New Zealand were also unsuccessful, although farmers were willing to load the potatoes they delivered to the quayside. The main effect of these strikebreaking efforts was to anger the Seamen's Union, which banned vessels carrying scabs. A series of union bans in other cities helped isolate Melbourne and secure victory for the strikers.

Inter-colonial action had been needed, said the Seamen, because the struggle had 'assumed a new phase, viz., Capital v. Labour.'[28] The great strikes of the 1890s were not far away. But the means of resolving the dispute pointed in quite another direction. After the return to work, Professor Kernot of Melbourne University convened a Board of Arbitration comprising equal numbers of management and union representatives, which granted most of the workers' demands. Bruce Smith no longer felt savage; he announced his delight with the peak union leadership, whom he found 'cool-headed, exceedingly amenable to reason'.[29] If the great strikes of the 1890s were on the horizon, so was the establishment of Australia's famous arbitration machinery.

Two other national organisations emerged in the second half of the decade. Under Spence's leadership, the AMA grew from the unification of local coal and metal mining unions. The AMA fought numerous, largely defensive, strikes in the years before 1890; the most important was the 1888 dispute in the coal fields of northern NSW.

Coal was vital for the ever-increasing numbers of steamships, railways and factories. Over the previous decade, coal production in the region had doubled, and the workforce had risen to 6,000; so this strike had a much greater social impact than earlier conflicts. The dispute concerned a union log of claims and employer demands to introduce a tributing (subcontracting) system. The AMA sent delegates throughout NSW to raise funds and rally support, while Victorian miners levied themselves a shilling per week. After violent confrontations with strikebreakers or 'blacklegs', strike leaders were arrested and charged with riot; the authorities even brought out a machine gun. The dispute ended with neither side clearly victorious, but it was memorable for the miners' manifesto, which showed hints of socialist thinking with its demand for 'the equal distribution of wealth'.[30]

Another significant dispute took place in Broken Hill. In November 1889, a one-week strike forced BHP to implement the closed shop. Broken Hill was on its way to becoming a centre of militancy. Here, however, the AMA was overshadowed by the Amalgamated Shearers' Union (ASU), founded in 1886, with Spence again prominent.

Three local shearers' unions already existed, in Moree, Wagga Wagga and Tasmania, but station owners seem to have provoked a general mobilisation by announcing a cut in the shearing rate. Angry letters poured in to country newspapers, and unions began to form around Young in eastern NSW, then at various places in the west of the colony. Next, Spence – along with David Temple – set up a shearers' union at Ballarat in Victoria. By July, South Australia had joined the movement. In August, Temple was in the Riverina organising shearers. By the end of the year, there was movement throughout Victoria, and attempts were in train to organise New Zealand. Not all efforts

AMALGAMATED SHEARERS' UNION OF AUSTRALASIA, ECHUCA VICTORIA, 1888

succeeded – Tasmania and New Zealand were disappointments – but, from 1887, the capitalists were facing unions across a vast stretch of eastern Australia. During disputes in 1887 and 1888, the ASU consolidated itself as a national organisation, defeating plans to cut the shearing rate.

Pastoralists themselves, gradually withdrawing from involvement in day-to-day shearing, stimulated unionisation on some parts of the wool track. A lot of stations, especially inland, were effectively run by managers or junior partners whom the workforce thought remote or arrogant. This occurred just at a time when shearers were beginning to get fed up with bossy managers. The legendary dissolute ex-convicts, capable of drinking a season's earnings in one debauch, were giving way to another type. The shearer of the 1870s and 1880s, commented itinerant writer Francis Adams, was 'a man who arrives on a horse, leading another' and who sent money home to his wife.[31] He expected the bosses to treat him with respect.

Yet, the union was actually strongest in far western NSW, where conditions were harsh, rations expensive, and the local union branch full of landless workers. Strike camps were large and easy to hold together. The Bourke branch was a key centre of militancy in the ASU. Here, most sheds accepted union demands or something close to them. In another type of area, where large numbers of small holding farmers sheared on a part-time basis, union consciousness was weak. Some smallholders owed the pastoralists money, so they feared antagonising them; others were fairly prosperous and therefore less interested in class struggle.

The Riverina and Victoria's western district saw bitter conflicts, with the union suffering defeats because of the availability of casual labour. In Victoria:

> The *Argus* featured 'Union Outrages' in almost unprecedented capitalized headlines. Camperdown was said to be in turmoil with many ugly scenes occurring. An 'assault on a station' – 'Woodlands', near Koroit – when the owner was 'seriously maltreated', the homestead defenders disarmed, and nine non-unionists captured, resulted in prolonged court cases; offenders were given severe sentences of imprisonment which were upset on appeal. The *Argus* discerned a link with the Kellys and a reaping of the fruits of the land laws.[32]

The following year, 1889, was quieter. Wool prices had risen, so the bosses preferred to avoid strife. Some employers became friendlier towards the union: in February 1889, several pastoralists and two of their associations attended its national conference. On the other hand, shearers in many places were accepting terms inferior to the ASU's official position.

The ASU officials themselves generally tried to avoid conflict – apart perhaps from W. W. Head, who 'subscribed to some ill-defined socialist beliefs and was far more inclined to confront pastoralists than to negotiate with them,'[33] the Australian Workers' Union (AWU) leaders were moderates. Spence himself was a Christian preacher, a member of the Creswick militia, prominent in the temperance movement and a justice of the peace who informed a Royal Commission that 'I do not believe in strikes at all.'[34] He believed that unionists:

> must demand the respect of capitalists to such an extent that the latter would ultimately come to the former and say, 'We will go mates on this or that concern.'[35]

Despite conciliatory tendencies on both sides, however, the showdown of the 1890s appears inevitable in retrospect.

Wages were not really the central issue. The *Australian Town and Country Journal* said of the notorious 1886 advertisement: 'A reduction of 2s 6d per hundred was not worth the trouble. The saving was too small to give relief.'[36]

Later, employers commonly offered good pay to shearers willing to accept the bosses' terms, in order to undermine the ASU. George Mair, bitter enemy of unions, thought that the shearing rate was:

> comparatively unimportant... The question is whether we shall preserve to ourselves the control of our business, or put ourselves under the rule of our own workmen.[37]

Certainly, the bosses also feared that, should they lose control, ruinous wage demands would follow. From 1889, the anti-union elements among pastoralists began to mobilise, and stronger employer organisations took shape.

The ASU's conciliatory stance was genuine. At the same time, however, its leaders saw collaboration with management as a means to institutionalise their presence in the industry and enforce the closed shop. This was incompatible with employer demands for 'freedom of contract'. For both sides, therefore, the key issue was who controlled the industry.

By 1890, pastoral unionism was losing momentum, and the bosses were becoming more aggressive. Union strength was also under threat from new shearing machines that made it easier to replace skilled shearers with novices. A concerned ASU leadership began looking to the maritime unions for assistance, as did the Queensland Shearers' Union (QSU), an independent body competing with the ASU. During a conflict over the closed shop at Jondaryan station on the Darling Downs, the Queenslanders explored the possibility of a port blockade to stop the transport of non-union wool. They also looked to the Australian Labor Federation (a force in Queensland, but virtually non-existent elsewhere) to organise solidarity.

The ASU likewise allied itself with the NSW maritime unions, ensuring that the Sydney Trades and Labor Council also fell into line, although some conservative elements would have preferred not to back the shearers. An ASU manifesto called on unionists 'to draw such a cordon around the Australian continent as will effectively prevent a bale of wool leaving unless shorn by union shearers.'[38] Ultimately, however, these initiatives were swallowed up in the great 1891 strikes. The Queensland union, as well as Spence and Temple, had hoped that the wool issue would remain isolated from other work on the wharves, which might allow the unions to divide the pastoral employers from the shipping companies. But the generalised conflict of 1891 was to have just the opposite effect.

The climate of worker optimism and union advance during the late 1880s had begun to breed solidarity across sectional boundaries. Although craft unions generally still guarded against incursions from the less skilled, craft barriers were not absolute. In 1886, workers in one of the NSW railways formed a single union open to porters, signal operators, guards and blacksmiths.

Around the same time, the 250-strong Mildura Land and Labour Union combined engineers, shed hands and unskilled grubbing gangs. It was more than symbolic unity: at times, skilled workers combined with grubbers in strikes to support shedhands' claims for higher pay.

One test for the quality of union solidarity was efforts to organise women. This was an area where sectional prejudice ran deep. NSW unions only tackled the task in the late 1880s, when union confidence was high. Yet the Boot Trade Union, established in August 1889, was open to both males and females; a male member later told the Commission on Strikes that the women's work was 'better done than the men could do it'. The TLC then attempted to create a tailoresses' union, holding an initial meeting of 30 workers. Peter Strong, former leader of the Tailors' Association, became the first president:

> Two years later Strong was to admit how he had fought against female labour for thirty years, and how it had only been during the late eighties that he had recognised the futility of the exercise. It was only then that he had set about trying to organise women workers.[39]

In 1890, the TLC established a general organising committee, which moved to organise laundresses and to create a Female Employees' Society. The laundresses struck in September 1891 over the sacking of a fellow worker. During the dispute, Creo Stanley, a socialist, became the first female delegate to the TLC, winning applause when she declared that she was 'not afraid of any man in the council; no, nor any press representative at the table yonder.'[40]

The Sydney unions also had many failings. Stanley resigned her seat five months later, protesting against the 'unmanly and insulting conduct of brother unionists'.[41] The Typographers declared women's membership unconstitutional, and even female-dominated industries were generally represented by male delegates on the TLC. In 1899, the TLC settled a dispute at Hirschman's factory in Redfern on terms that excluded women from the union. However, only a small majority approved this decision, which quickly provoked criticism in the pages of *The Worker*.

The General Labourers' Union, allied with the ASU, sought to organise women workers in Sydney, Melbourne and a number of country centres, while Rose Summerville worked with tailoresses, domestic servants and boot trade employees. Unfortunately, these efforts were not very successful, and misfortune overwhelmed them in the crisis years of the 1890s.

3.
CRISIS AND INCORPORATION

LABOUR IN THE 1890S

The 1890s brought economic depression and a vast confrontation between capital and labour. But how closely were economic and industrial developments linked?

Labour historian Brian Fitzpatrick suggested that great industrial battles began in 1890 because:

> this was the time at which, a long period of prosperity having unmistakably closed, capitalists decided that the time for making concessions to the unions had closed also.[1]

Actually, social conflicts and economic turning points are seldom quite so neatly juxtaposed.

Raw growth figures for Australia as a whole do show the economy peaking in 1889; but, once these are adjusted for inflation, the peak shifts to 1891. Stuart Svensen argues that pastoralists' profits were holding up well in the run-up to the great strikes.[2]

Apparently, the onset of depression came after the strikes commenced. On the other hand, the years preceding them were full of danger signs. There was certainly a recession in Victoria, where the land boom collapsed, and employment began to fall. Even in NSW, the jobless rate rose to 4.7 percent in 1891 and 7.6 percent among the industrial work force.[3]

The very discrepancy between GDP trends in current and constant prices reflects the onset of significant disinflation, usually a sign of recession. There was excess capacity in much of industry – two rival shipping cartels were locked in a ruinous price war – while the unions were pursuing aggressive wage claims. These facts undoubtedly encouraged capital to take a harder line with organised labour in 1890, and depression conditions eventually made it possible for them to thoroughly crush union aspirations.

THE 1890 MARITIME STRIKE

Two conflicts loom large when we talk about how the maritime strike started: the clash at the Jondaryan shearing shed and attempts by marine officers to organise. Jondaryan, as we have seen, was not so much about money as about control of the work process. This was also true of the marine officers' dispute.

These officers had been asking for better pay and conditions for six years with little result. They were now demanding a £2 pay rise but would have settled for half that. The money was not a major problem for the steamship companies, the largest of which actually conceded a £1 rise in July 1890. What became the key issue for the employers was the Marine Officers' Association (MOA) decision to affiliate with the Victorian THC. The MOA's members were, after all, ships' officers. Affiliation with the THC might mean their involvement in wider industrial disputes, on the side of the workers. This could jeopardise employer control.

It is true that the Marine Engineers had long been affiliated with the union movement, and the MOA's affiliation had not mattered much to their employers a couple of weeks before. The MOA had sought to allay any fears – that's why it had joined the THC rather than the Maritime Council, a separate body where it would have been more directly linked to other maritime unions. Despite these efforts, the ship owners provoked their strike with a fairly insulting letter, after failing to goad them into industrial action on a different issue two days earlier. On this basis, Svensen presents the affiliation as 'a pseudo-issue', a pretext for employers keen to provoke a conflict.[4] That only makes sense if we focus narrowly on the machinations of a cabal of ship owners. Against the background of a wider class mobilisation on both sides, this clash of management and union rights takes on considerable symbolic importance.

If two apparently unrelated disputes, Jondaryan and the marine officers, awakened very similar fears in the capitalist mind, this flowed from the scale and perceived ambitions of the Australian labour movement. In employer circles, there was worried talk of 'federated labour'. What they meant was not so much the politically inspired Australian Labour Federation (never operational outside Queensland), but rather the conspicuous growth of industrial solidarity in practice – demonstrated by the 1888 maritime dispute and the port blockade over Jondaryan. They also worried about the rise of a national labour leadership:

> an employer had only to touch the lamp of trade unionism and out popped that evil genie, William Guthrie Spence. He seemed to be omnipresent – hovering over the miners, the shearers, the general labourers, and now the waterfront.[5]

Such developments seemed to raise the spectre of a general strike, or even social revolution. So, naturally, they made the employers more open to the idea of systematic organisation of their own.

Before 1890, employer organisation was still somewhat fragmentary, so we cannot meaningfully ask what the capitalists as a class 'decided' to do in 1890. The extensive mobilisation of the bourgeoisie behind a coherent leadership and, somewhat later, a fighting program was a product of circumstances, political argument and manoeuvre. Capitalist attitudes were initially quite diverse, partly reflecting different economic conditions. Among most groups of employers, as among the pastoralists, there were those who accepted unionism and those who loathed it, with a majority willing to go either way for commercial advantage. Some industries were better placed to fight a strike: most importantly, the ship owners presided over a compact and cartelised industry, so they represented a kind of strike force.

In NSW, class divisions were often raw and bitter. They were less so in Victoria, where owners of small manufacturing firms were still close to their working-class origins, protectionist ideology had convinced sections of the labour movement that the employers were their friend, and liberal politicians owed their seats to workers' votes. Consequently, the strike was less bitter in Victoria. However, by the late 1880s, things were changing in Victoria, too, as manufacturing firms grew larger and employers more arrogant. The Victorian Employers' Union, prodded by the anti-union boot manufacturer John Mair, was reconsidering its original support for the colony's industrial Board of Conciliation at the time the strike broke out. During the strike itself, Victorian employers took a fairly hard line.

Despite the factors pushing capitalists towards a united stance, they could not have held together without a minority of hawks taking leadership. The most important was master stevedore Alfred Lamb. Lamb owned one of the main firms loading wool for export, served as a vice-president of the NSW Employers' Union and was MLA for West Sydney. He collected signatures on a document committing stevedores to load non-union wool and prevailed on them to put up a cash bond to back up the commitment. Lamb, who was also close to the leadership of the Pastoralists' Union of NSW, next persuaded key members of that body to pledge exclusive support to those stevedores who had signed his agreement. After locking in some other, additional players, he travelled to Melbourne and repeated the procedure. Meanwhile, the shipowners were assembling a £20,000 defence fund.

This was an exercise in conscious class organisation, probably based on lessons drawn from the labour movement. There were still doubters, even important ones like Jesse Gregson, superintendent of the AAC, but Gregson's reservations were mainly about timing. There were sectors of industry not yet drawn into the alliance, such as the coal owners. Employers in Victoria and South Australia were generally less aggressive than the hard core of NSW capitalists. However, the actual outbreak of the dispute and the events of the first few weeks were to overcome most of the remaining hesitation. When mine workers refused to supply coal to scab vessels, the coal owners promptly locked them out. Employer-organised public meetings were well attended, and the bosses' confidence rose steadily.

As they gained ascendancy in the dispute, the bosses began to focus on a single slogan: freedom of contract. The issue had, of course, been on many individual capitalists' minds, and they had used the term in previous disputes. Now it became a triumphant and vindictive rallying cry. Rickard notes:

> From the point of view of the trade unions the calamity of 1890 was that it provided employers with the key for their policy for the next decade.[6]

The union leaders weren't looking for a strike, any more than they had been eager for any of the major confrontations during the 1880s. They seemed to have no choice; the events unfolded remorselessly. The ASU leadership believed its membership to be shaky and saw the closed shop as the only way to shore it up. Temple and Spence hoped that the mere threat of port blockades, as in the Jondaryan case, would be enough to bring about a settlement without the need for any real industrial mobilisation.

This strategy relied on keeping the wool issue separate from other grievances concerning the maritime unions. In the event, the alliance between unionists of port and bush actually helped to bring on a general conflict, while also uniting the employers. The MOA would have accepted any reasonable settlement; the trouble was that, by mid-August, the employers no longer wanted one. A belligerent anti-union letter from the ship owners convinced the marine officers to break off negotiations.

As ships came into port, marine officers and seamen walked off them, and waterside workers joined the stoppage. Other groups of workers either were locked out or stopped work in solidarity. The struggle would eventually involve around 50,000 Australian unionists and 10,000 New Zealanders.

Although the union leaders did not want the strike, and many worried privately about the consequences, there was still an initial mood of confidence in labour ranks. The impressive growth of working-class organisation, as well as the general climate of public sympathy for the labour cause, had boosted workers' hopes and alarmed employers. Unfortunately, union organisation also had serious weaknesses. Numbers had risen rapidly, and the unions had made gains, but the newer unions lacked experience and discipline. Only the coal miners had much recent experience with prolonged strikes. The image of strong, even dictatorial, centralised organisation was a mirage. The outbreak of hostilities at the waterfront caught Spence himself unawares. 'I have often wondered how it was I knew nothing about it at the time,' he later remarked, 'but I was taken by surprise to hear the officers had walked out.'[7] An Inter-colonial Labour Conference didn't convene until 12 September, by which time the strike was well on its way to defeat.

At the same time, those sections of public opinion represented by the middle classes and liberal elements of the bourgeoisie were much less reliably pro-labour than either unionists or employers had realised. Capitalists discovered the power of law-and-order agitation to mobilise the middle layers of society for reactionary ends and at least neutralise the liberals. The supposedly pro-union Melbourne *Age* portrayed the strike as 'an unarmed insurrection of class against class',[8] while Victorian authorities seized on a gas workers' strike to orchestrate panic about what criminals might get up to in the dark streets. Previously, society's middle layers had often sympathised with labour, especially in Victoria; now, the prospect of general class warfare made them more open to law-and-order sentiments. This supplied the political basis for such liberal politicians as Henry Parkes and Alfred Deakin to deploy troops against the strikers.

Most dangerous of all was the availability of 'free labour'. Some of this came from the middle classes or from recent arrivals in the colonies with no local loyalties. But others were unemployed workers, mainly unskilled, whom the unions had too often ignored. That respectable institution, the Melbourne Trades Hall, stood conspicuously aloof from the frequent waves of agitation among the unemployed; it was left to socialists and anarchists to organise thousands of jobless workers at Queen's Wharf at the start of August 1890. Perhaps the Trades Hall found this element too radical – the demonstrators did indeed try to throw a police contingent into the harbour. But the unions might have done more to organise the unskilled and build relations with the unemployed; they were to pay a high price for their failures. One employer after another found scabs to replace unionists on the job.

Support for the union cause flowed from as far away as London, where dockers, remembering how Australian donations had helped their strike in 1889, raised £15,000–20,000, and 4,000 people rallied in Victoria Park. Far greater crowds gathered in Australian centres. The greatest crowd came together in Melbourne on 31 August. Between 50,000 and 100,000 people, in a city of 400,000, assembled at Flinders Park. Despite the best efforts of radical agitators at the fringe, it was a highly respectable gathering, with much talk from the main platform about

SPECIAL CONSTABLES MOBILISED FOR THE MARITIME STRIKE, SYDNEY, 1890

the virtues of arbitration and even the right of blacklegs to work unmolested. The bourgeoisie were undoubtedly relieved; they had been fretting about possible disturbances. On the previous day, Colonel Tom Price had assembled 200 armed troopers and issued a notorious instruction:

> I do not think your aid will be required, but if it is, let there be no half measures with what you do…if the order is given to fire, don't let me see one rifle pointed up in the air. Fire low and lay them out.[9]

Price later claimed that he was only citing government regulations, which did in fact require troops to fire low. Union supporters still took his words as demonstrating the authorities' capacity for partisan violence. The state was certainly mobilising its repressive forces against them: by the end of the strike, 3,283 special constables had been sworn in, drawn overwhelmingly from the middle classes – company clerks, managers and upper-level public servants. Price's ancestry made him an ideal symbol of repression: his father was John Giles Price, the sadistic Norfolk Island prison commandant killed by a crowd of convicts at Williamstown in 1857.

Rallies and processions in Sydney were smaller, yet still sizeable, with the Australian Socialist League providing a radical political edge. An initial march only attracted some 7,000 participants; but it was followed a week later by what the *Sydney Morning Herald* called 'one of the largest displays of the kind yet seen in Australia'. The lower portion of George Street was:

> filled by a seething mass of humanity. It seemed as though all Sydney were out to participate in or gaze upon the spectacle of labour defying capital.

Contingents from all the trades seemed to be on the march, which extended for a mile and a half. The anti-union *Herald* was quick to claim that 'from the many thousands of sightseers there were no manifestations of sympathy', reporting that a large majority of the members of the Sydney Stock Exchange had joined the Employers' Union, along with 'the Associated Warehousemen in a body'.[10] Whatever the exact distribution of public sentiment, this was a sharply polarised city.

It was a fitting climate for a group of leading Sydney employers to stage their greatest provocation: the transport of wool through Sydney streets to Circular Quay on 19 September. Trolleymen and draymen had struck and engaged in some determined picketing but had not stopped the employers transporting wool by barge from Darling Harbour. 'A work-gang of wool-brokers, auctioneers, squatters, bankers, lawyers, lackeys and millionaires...in morning suits, top hats and lemon gloves', assisted by special constables, drove ten trolleys of wool to the Quay among wild scenes.

Thousands lined the streets and stared from windows, many hurling abuse and missiles. Finally, mounted troopers forcibly dispersed a crowd at Circular Quay itself. The aim was apparently to provoke a riot, leading to the arrest of strike leaders, and perhaps to bring about the deployment of British troops from visiting warships against the unionists; but the union leaders were not involved in the riot, and the latter parts of the scheme came to nothing.[11] As a matter of fact, given the size of the conflict, the amount of violence on the part of unionists throughout the strike was fairly low, a fact attested by the NSW Inspector-General of Police.[12]

By this time, the unions were already on their way to defeat. Calling out the NSW shearers in late September was an act of desperation. Thousands of unionists who had already made generous donations to strike funds now responded gallantly to the call, but they paid a terrible price in lost wages and victimisation. Thousands of others found ways to avoid conflict with the employers. Either way, it made little difference to the result. On 31 October, the marine officers informed the Melbourne Trades Hall that they were withdrawing from membership, and different sections of the union movement threw in the towel at different times over the next two months. Some miners did not return to work until January 1891.

CONTINUING CONFLICT

As the strike front crumbled, hawkish employers set about imposing the cruellest of terms. Bosses refused even to talk to union leaders; militants endured victimisation; workers had to disavow their union to get a chance of employment; and even scabs sometimes suffered as the delights of 'freedom of contract' descended on the colonies. 'Free labourers' working for the Australasian United Steam Navigation Company went on strike in both Brisbane and Sydney over pay cuts, as did a group of blackleg miners at Mt Kembla.

The leading employers' merciless stance provoked further changes in outlook among the middle-class and liberal elements of the bourgeoisie. Calls from newspapers and politicians for the bosses to moderate their position had little impact on the course of the dispute, but they lent impetus to the growing sentiment for institutionalised conciliation and arbitration.

Squabbling and recriminations were common in labour's ranks in the face of defeat. By October, the strike leadership in Sydney was already spending much of its time in personal altercations. In the Melbourne THC, the rank and file accused Trenwith of withholding information, while NSW shearers complained of bureaucratic mismanagement and a situation where 'fat billets are made for secretaries, delegates, reps and their hosts of relatives'.[13] There was nothing inherently left wing about these criticisms from the members; in fact, the shearers were complaining about having to go on strike. However, there are some indications that rank-and-file activists showed greater militancy than the union officials during the maritime strike. J. H. Storey, president of the Sydney Chamber of Commerce, told his annual meeting that 'the [union] men themselves seem disposed to even throw over their own leaders to achieve their ends.'[14]

The defeat of 1890 was severe, yet by no means absolute. In some places, the unions gained membership in the aftermath. The NSW TLC reported 'a steady persistent advocacy of Unionism which must bear fruit as soon as the existing depression passes away,'[15] while the ASU leaders were still arguing in 1891 that a full season of shearing would allow the union to rebuild its position. Some workers had actually won victories. These included Broken Hill miners and some of the Adelaide unions; they were benefiting from a temporary economic upswing caused by the rapid development of the Broken Hill mines, and their position was not yet undermined by unemployment. There were also small

WOMEN'S BRIGADE ASSAULTING SCABS BROKEN HILL 1892

shipping companies along the east coast that came to terms with the unions, in order to seize market share from their bigger rivals.

It was the severe depression that decisively weakened the union movement, by creating mass unemployment. Even so, the organised workers put up stiff resistance to attacks on wages and conditions in a series of further disputes: the Queensland shearers' strike of 1891, the 1892 Broken Hill disputes, the 1893 seamen's strike and the shearing dispute strike of 1894 were all bitterly fought, even though they mostly ended in union defeats.

The Queensland dispute was, in some ways, a repeat of the maritime strike, in which Queensland shearers had not been involved. By mid-September 1890, once the outcome of the maritime strike could be clearly foreseen, pastoralists in the northern colony began mobilising under the leadership of George Fairbairn. Once again, they focused on issues of control. They took exception to QSU policies which embraced right of entry for union organisers and which demanded that shearers alone decide whether sheep were too wet to shear. The employers also wanted wage cuts and 'freedom of contract'. The QSU and the allied Queensland Labourers' Union (QLU) would not accept these terms.

Unfortunately for the unions, the strike began early in 1891. General shearing was not until July. The unions considered accepting the bosses' terms for a few months, then repudiating the agreement in July, but decided that this was politically unviable. The consequence, however, was that unionists had begun to exhaust their resources before the most important part of the shearing season. They were also up against a steady flow of strikebreakers, especially from Melbourne – where unemployment was high – and a massive show of force by the Queensland government. Finally, fundraising efforts were disappointing, with southern workers less able to help after their own defeats.

Weeks of frustration in strike camps led to minor cases of violence, which the authorities seized on as an excuse for repression. In March 1891, group of strikers at Clermont jostled and abused four employer officials; arrests ensued, and more police and soldiers arrived. Later in the month, the main strike leaders at Barcaldine were arrested. By 4 April, there had been 61 arrests,

SHEARERS' STRIKE CAMP, HUGHENDEN QLD, 1891

and more followed. Eleven unionists received sentences of three years with hard labour. By April, defeat was staring the shearers in the face. Divisions emerged in their ranks, with one section calling for more aggressive tactics, and others drifting back to work. Some sections of the Carriers' Union decided not to strike. By June, the last shearers were throwing in the towel.

The Queensland events were rich in symbolism. The romance of mounted and armed shearers, some talking revolution, is compelling to this day, although the vast majority of the strikers were determinedly non-violent. More significantly, it was here that the capitalist state showed its full repressive power. Up to 2,000 troops, police and special constables entered the fray, but this still wasn't enough to satisfy some. Judge George Rogers Harding, presiding at the trial after the Clermont events, criticised police for not firing on strikers: 'There would not have been many who boo-hooed the second time if I had been one of them,' announced Harding. When a defence lawyer objected: 'You can't shoot a man for disorderly conduct,' Harding retorted: 'Very probably they could find justification.'[16] Around the time of this trial, Henry Lawson's verse appeared, warning that workers ought not be blamed 'if blood should stain the wattle'.[17]

Despite deteriorating economic conditions, the unions did better in the 1894 strike which embraced Queensland, NSW, South Australia and Victoria – all, by that time, under the banner of the AWU, uniting shearers and labourers. This dispute saw more violence than the earlier ones, with unionists acutely aware by now of what they were up against and, sometimes, feeling fairly desperate. At one shed, police and strikers exchanged 40 rounds of rifle file. A worker died. River steamers transporting strike-breakers became targets for attack, culminating on the night of 6 August with the seizure of the *Rodney*, which militants burnt to the waterline. Abductions of scabs and brawls in country towns were commonplace. Colonial governments intervened repeatedly on the employers' side.

REMOVING SHEARERS DURING SHEARERS' STRIKE, QUEENSLAND, 1891

While the Queensland section of the AWU pulled out of the strike relatively early, the traditionally strongest branches of the union in western NSW and western Victoria gave the pastoralists a stiffer fight than expected. Their timing was also better than in 1891, because the call-out in these areas came at the time of general shearing. Some employers had chastening experiences with incompetent 'free labourers' and had to accommodate the unions. There were numerous compromise agreements. Even though the strike eventually petered out, it was probably a partial victory for the AWU because it halted the momentum of employer attacks for a time. Unfortunately, steadily worsening unemployment over the next few years made further falls in wages and declines in union membership inevitable, in what Spence called the 'dark days' of the AWU.[18]

Meanwhile, Broken Hill unions had taken a hammering. BHP had locked out its miners during the maritime strike, ostensibly because of transport difficulties. Unionists thought that employers were punishing them for raising funds in support of the strikers and accused them of insider trading (dumping shares before the lockout, then buying them back on the cheap). However, it may simply have been a matter of backing up fellow capitalists or of straightforward material interest – BHP management had financial links to other key employers. Management soon paid a price for its actions: not only did 5,000 unionists meet to protest; not only did local business call for an end to the lockout; but shareholders were horrified to see a stoppage while silver prices were high. The bosses retreated, and the unions pressed home their advantage, pushing up wages and cutting the working week from 48 to 46 hours.

By 1892, however, silver prices were falling. The mine owners were ready to ruthlessly enforce 'freedom of contract'. They scrapped all agreements with the unions, provoking a four-month strike. Workers' organisations were thoroughly smashed amid fierce repression – at one point, police with fixed bayonets surrounded the union headquarters – and several strike leaders served time in prison. A year later, the seamen failed to resist savage wage cuts, their strike broken within a month by repression and blacklegs.

With trade unionism badly weakened and the depression deepening, the unemployed staged desperate actions. Crowds of ragged jobless gathered regularly at Melbourne's Queen's Wharf or Sydney's Domain. No longer confined to a fringe element in a few slum neighbourhoods, as the unemployed had been during the 1880s, the crowds became more assertive. They marched in the streets, gathering numbers in industrial suburbs and then invading the city centres:

> Bearing banners by day and torches by night, they transformed the city into an arena of social conflict. Often they marched in military formation... In May 1892 Melbourne's unemployed, the self-styled 'Second Victorian

Regiment' attempted to storm the steps of parliament... Other demonstrators forced their way through the bishop's gardens, marched on the Governor's residence, and harangued representatives of the Chamber of Commerce and the Salvation Army.[19]

Melbourne's wives and mothers marched on the city's parliamentary buildings, pleading for work for their husbands and sons and also demanding work for themselves, besieging the labour bureau and asserting their right to register. In September:

> police noted the effect three female orators had upon a crowd gathered outside St Paul's Cathedral... Their audience numbered 600 people, at least fifty of whom were women.[20]

The new Labor MPs offered precious little help. W. A. Trenwith, whose election campaign had appealed specifically to the jobless, forgot about them once in office. When questioned, he said that the government should be approached 'in the proper spirit'; when this provoked outrage, he pontificated about the 'indecent excesses' of unemployed demonstrators.[21]

The unemployed, on their own, couldn't sustain an effective political movement and were sometimes diverted into destructive dead ends. Anarchist proposals to solve the employment crisis by bombing rich people's homes were relatively harmless, as long as no one acted on them. The same couldn't be said for 400 women who marched along Melbourne's Russell Street, 'tapping rather heavily with their umbrellas at the glass windows and doors... of Chinese laundries' and 'loudly groaning' at any Chinese they passed.[22] These were symptoms of weakness and despair in the wake of labour's defeat.

Why had the unions lost so many strikes so badly? Economic conditions were an important factor, especially in the later disputes. Unionists also reflected on their failure to adequately organise the unorganised or establish solidarity with the unemployed. But the greatest issues, in union activists' minds,

UNION LEADERS IMPRISONED AFTER THE 1891 SHEARER'S STRIKE, BARCALDINE QUEENSLAND

were politics and the state. Governments claimed to be a neutral party upholding the law, but they had stepped in to back the employers again and again. Even supposed 'friends of labour' among liberal MPs had supported this. A minority of politicised workers was turning to radical politics, and the emergence of the Labor Party was at hand – a topic dealt with in detail in other publications.[23] In industry, another solution became a fad: institutionalised arbitration.

'THIS KNOCK-KNEED THING'

Schemes for resolving industrial disputes were nothing new, and neither were plans to regulate wages and conditions – but they had always met resistance from unions and employers alike. The crisis of the 1890s, which unleashed a hunt for solutions to social problems, made both sides think again. In NSW, Henry Parkes embraced arbitration for the first time, even giving his Royal Commission on Strikes terms of reference that pointed in that direction. By the middle of the decade, serious moves were underway. Some colonies relied on factory legislation and wages boards, while NSW adopted the arbitration system that became the national model after federation. A look at Victoria and NSW will highlight differences and demonstrate important elements of common ground.

The Victorian system emerged from campaigns against sweating. Victoria had more women and children working in factories, and the depression had both increased the numbers and worsened their conditions. This horrified respectable society, from genuine humanitarians to stuffy moralists who thought it improper for females to work in industry. Accordingly, the Turner government's *Factory Act* regulated labour and provided for a minimum wage in certain industries. Wages boards, comprising elected employer and employee representatives, were to administer this under a supposedly neutral chair. The Act was modest in scope but important in its longer-term implications, because Labor MP George Prendergast successfully moved to extend the minimum wage to males, and the wages boards were later extended to other industries.

Being very popular, the reforms went through with a minimum of fuss, despite obstruction from the Upper House and sections of employers. Although Trades Hall was supportive, the reforms, like the anti-sweating movement itself, were not primarily a labour initiative. Leading Anti-Sweating League figures included clergymen and respectable ladies full of condescending devotion to the downtrodden. Similarly, it was liberal middle-class politicians who pushed through the Factory Acts. Colonial liberals had previously shied away from state intervention, but many changed their minds in the 1890s.

While some capitalists resisted the boards, others accepted or even supported them – well over 100 employers in the cigar, saddlery, marble mason, printing and tanning trades signed petitions in their favour. Country employers were generally exempted and therefore did not object, while some urban manufacturers had good grounds to endorse reform. Free trade interests had long argued that tariff protection fostered uncompetitive sweatshops, claims that grew louder among the misery of the 1890s, so manufacturers sought to deflect criticism by championing regulation and the minimum wage. Some hoped, in fact, that a minimum wage might discipline their less scrupulous competitors.

Manufacturers also looked to the labour movement as a political ally. They lacked the social prestige and institutionalised political power (through the Upper House, for example) enjoyed by pastoral or financial capital and, consequently, needed the voting base that labour supplied. This was especially important with federation on the horizon and with tactical manoeuvres already underway to set the tariff policies of a future federal government.

Some writers see the wages boards as the outcome of an alliance between male workers, employers and the arbitration system to disadvantage women.[24] The argument is that the arbitration system entrenched gender divisions and the family wage in ways that benefited male workers to the detriment of females. Males monopolised skilled jobs and used the family wage concept to exclude females from 'male' jobs generally. This argument presumes that male unionists exercised power and could enforce their will. But that wasn't the case.

Firstly, although arbitration embraced and reproduced sexism like other social institutions, gender divisions were hardly something new. Almost everyone took them for granted, including those who suffered most. Secondly, skilled jobs were a small sector of the labour market which most men couldn't enter either. Thirdly, male tradesmen were not very successful at excluding women. Moreover, exclusionary tactics weren't always directed at women, being also used to exclude male Chinese or to limit the number of men and boys entering particular trades; nor were they exclusively masculine:

> It is well known that tailoresses were elitist in their attitude toward other women workers in the clothing industry... As Frances points out, dressmakers and milliners saw themselves as 'artists rather than craftswomen'. Separate unions existed for stock and order hands until 1897. Outworkers were excluded from these unions on the grounds that members 'did not want to be dragged down to the outworkers' level'.[25]

One reason the Tailoresses' Association declined is that, when employers responded to higher factory wages by using more outworkers, the union floundered. Hostility to outworkers who were undermining wage rates led to irrational refusals to admit them to the union. The Tailoresses' Association repeated the error of male crafts, who sought to preserve an elite status by excluding women and the unskilled from jobs and unions. Far from reflecting union power, sectional divisions were both a symptom and a cause of union weakness. The same was true of arbitration itself, which took root nationally in the wake of major union defeats.

The birth of arbitration was no more difficult in NSW than Victoria, although forms and processes differed. Premier George Reid dominated the parliament for several years with Labor support, after fighting a demagogic 1895 election campaign around what were actually very modest proposals for land taxation and reform of the Upper House. In 1899, Labor switched its support to his rivals, and the Reid government fell. But the *Arbitration Act 1901* represented the end of a process begun by Parkes a decade earlier, a process not really the property of any one parliamentary faction.

The Labor Party did play a greater role in establishing arbitration in NSW than in Victoria, but it was generally a stronger force in NSW. Initially, the industrial labour movement expressed considerable opposition to the whole idea – resistance from both capital and labour was stronger in class-polarised NSW. The unions that generally favoured it were those attempting to organise large, far-flung groups of workers employed on a temporary basis (shearers and maritime workers) or with particular local traditions (coal miners) or facing intense antagonism from the employer (the railways).

Most urban unions were not enthusiastic. They had opposed non-compulsory arbitration bills in 1882 and 1888. Industrial defeat undoubtedly increased union support for regulated settlement of disputes, just as it reduced enthusiasm from employers who now felt able to dominate the industrial scene. But the unions still held back from support for a similar bill in 1892 and soon felt vindicated: the 1892 Act lost credibility in union eyes when the employers refused to submit the Broken Hill strike to its machinery.

Leftists such as W. G. Higgs, editor of the *Australian Workman*, and TLC delegates Jamie Moroney and John Dwyer led the opposition inside the labour movement; and in 1900, the socialist journal *People and Collectivist* was still warning:

when this knock-kneed thing has become law, the class war will still go on; the worker will still be robbed of the major portion of the wealth he creates; and his great concern is not how he might temporise with the robber... his great concern is rather how to get rid of the robber.[26]

Not until 1898 did NSW Labor include arbitration in its fighting program. By this time, the Labor Party was in the hands of the AWU and urban politicians – some of the latter with a socialist background but increasingly remote from the rank and file. The Labor Party elements who helped introduce arbitration were thus somewhat similar to the middle-class reformers of Victoria or the lawyers who populated all colonial parliaments.

Those union officials who backed arbitration often did so out of a conservative impulse. Aware of worker bitterness after the great strikes, they feared that, without institutions to channel industrial disputes, the next upheaval 'would be perfectly impossible for any leaders to control'.[27] It appears that, by the 1890s, Australian labour already displayed that tension between conservative leaders and rank-and-file rebels which is so common in trade union movements. Antonio Gramsci explained:

> [Under capitalism] when individuals are only valued as owners of commodities, which they trade as property, the workers too are forced to obey the iron laws of general necessity; they become traders in their sole property – their labour power and professional skills. More exposed to the risks of competition, the workers have accumulated their property in ever broader and more comprehensive 'firms', they have created these enormous apparatuses for the concentration of work energy, they have imposed prices and hours and disciplined the market. They have hired from outside or produced from inside a trusted administrative staff expert in this kind of speculation, able to dominate market conditions, to lay down contracts, to evaluate commercial risks and to initiate profitable economic operations.

[T]he union bureaucrat conceives industrial legality as a permanent state of affairs. He too often defends it from the same point of view as the proprietor. He sees only chaos and wilfulness in everything that emerges from the working masses. He does not understand the worker's act of rebellion against capitalist discipline.[28]

As in Victoria, NSW capitalists were divided, with some in the countryside prepared to support arbitration. The hardliners who had mobilised the employing class during the maritime strike couldn't repeat their success on this occasion. The employers' disarray found expression in the contradictory and opportunistic arguments the anti-arbitration forces put forward around the turn of the century. They opposed federal legislation as 'an encroachment upon the rights of the States', yet they thought the NSW legislation undesirable 'inasmuch as conciliation and arbitration...is specifically reserved in the Federal Constitution for the Federal Parliament'. Having made voluntary arbitration unworkable, they nevertheless opposed compulsion on the grounds that 'voluntary arbitration worked extremely well'.[29]

Arbitration and Victorian-style wages boards were originally seen as incompatible alternatives, with the former understood as a mechanism for settling disputes rather than for regulation. However, just as the wages boards grew far beyond their original domain, so arbitration expanded to include awards that set wages and conditions. In both colonies, moves to institutionalise class collaboration pointed towards the introduction of the aged pension and assistance to the unemployed; critics of labour market regulation warned that it would create unemployment, especially among older workers. In both colonies, arbitration also encouraged wider organisation of both capital and labour, because neither wages boards nor arbitration tribunals could deal with each workplace or employee separately. Dozens of new unions sprang up, including some bogus outfits sponsored by employers, and the capitalists' own organisations flourished as well.

In neither colony – nor anywhere in Australia – did wages boards or arbitration achieve much for workers. Bosses found endless ways to safeguard their interests. When the wages board for the Victorian fellmongering industry fixed standard hours at 48 per week, all its employer representatives resigned. After an ensuing court battle went against them, most of the employers closed their businesses and sacked their employees. As a consequence, the *Factories and Shops Continuance Act 1902* effectively gave the bosses a right of veto. Moreover, the Victorian system gave no special place to trade unionists. Non-union employees also served on the boards. Employers might even pressure worker representatives; in fact, four out of five employee members of the jam industry board lost their jobs after voting to increase wages.

Arbitration did give the unions formal standing; but this was a mixed blessing for workers, because it also further increased the authority of the full-time officials, who were becoming increasingly dominant in the union movement. Billy Hughes, for example, emerged as the dominant figure in the Wharf Labourers' Union and sought to confine its efforts to the arbitration system rather than taking strike action. Hughes hoped that the federal Arbitration Court would 'enforce upon the men the very necessary lesson that unionism has responsibilities'.[30]

The Commonwealth *Conciliation and Arbitration Act 1904* didn't establish any wage-fixing principles based on gender. The Arbitration Court itself established these, through cases such as the 1907 Harvester Judgement and the Fruitpickers' Case, in which Justice Higgins established a 'family wage' benchmark. Contrary to the conventional view, which blamed organised labour for gender discrimination, the union demanded equal pay in the Fruitpickers' Case – but Justice Higgins decided otherwise, on the grounds that a man had to support a family.

Arbitration and the wages boards were neither a bosses' plot nor a triumph for the labour movement. Rather, they were the institutional form for social peace which emerged from the crisis of the 1890s. It's no mystery, from the Marxist perspective, that neither of the two main classes in society made the running in the debates around industrial regulation and wage fixing, with the initiative falling instead to middle layers: liberal reformers, professional politicians, full-time trade union officials. These are precisely the elements that most yearn for industrial peace.

With no consistent opposition from either capitalists or workers, they were able to shape institutions for administering and preserving capitalist industrial relations. That included, of course, the ultimate power of the boss – for, as the employers reminded that great advocate of arbitration, Alfred Deakin: 'The fundamental principle of our social system is inequality, and on that its health depends.'[31]

4.
GENDER, CLASS AND THE ROAD TO WOMEN'S SUFFRAGE

'Votes for women' was one of the great causes of the late 19th and early 20th centuries. We won it in Australia relatively early. Yet, after years of campaigning finally achieved it, women's suffrage had relatively little impact on our society. To understand why, we need to look once again at class forces.

Between 1860 and 1890, the dynamic of Australia's capitalist development reshaped gender relations: in some ways limiting women's rights, but in other ways creating important new opportunities. Theoretically, the nuclear family reigned supreme. Amongst the social elite, this assigned women a rather peculiar role, which Beverley Kingston describes:

> The complex business of maintaining caste, status, and hierarchy in society, of ensuring that marriages were arranged that were suitable or advantageous to the family, the business or the property, of celebrating the birth of heirs,

entertaining the right people, or keeping the close-knit circles of family and friends fully functioning, was, in the hands of a capable woman, as important and impressive as her husband's political, diplomatic, or entrepreneurial activity.[1]

The middle classes, as well as the craft unionists and their families who aspired to middle-class status, also defined female roles in domestic terms. The jumped-up shopkeeper Henry Parkes declared a woman's 'high and honourable destiny' to be duty in the home, because 'men rule in commerce, in the market and in the state'.[2] The fact that his uncertain business only survived because of Clarinda Parkes' capabilities was not enough to free his mind from dogma.

However, social changes were beginning to challenge the family institution. Mass production eroded traditional crafts and dashed the middle-class aspirations of the craftsmen. New factories produced simple household items such as bread and candles, which housewives and daughters had previously made at home, creating pressures and incentives for women to go out to work. Demands mounted for liberalised divorce laws, and more couples, mainly in the middle class, began practising birth control in the 1870s. Within 15 years, this caused a conspicuous fall in the birth rate, which accelerated in the economic depression of the 1890s. These trends aroused fears of 'race suicide' that persisted well into the next century, becoming the subject of a NSW Royal Commission in 1903–04.

The gender imbalance declined steadily in the second half of the century. In Victoria, the number of females was 64 percent of the number of males in 1861, but it had risen to 91 percent two decades later and was virtually at par in Melbourne. This eroded a long-standing obstacle to marriage for men, but it began to create one for some women: while males were now more likely to find marriage partners, females (especially Irish immigrants) were less likely to do so. Matrimony was no longer automatic for females. At the same time, greater job and even career opportunities began to open up, attracting women away from supposedly natural domestic bliss.

Even in the most conservative decades, there had always been some successful female participants in commerce and the labour force, including pockets where they worked on equal terms with men. These tended to be in places where the family unit was also a productive unit, such as farms. On a small selection, there was less scope to divide the 'public' and 'private' spheres.

TRADE UNIONIST AND LABOR POLITICIAN, W.G. SPENCE

Women who had been equal partners running farms might also find themselves running local post offices. Postmistresses earning equal salaries were common in colonial NSW, both in country towns and Sydney suburbs. Their husbands, who therefore had an economic interest in equal pay, supported their careers, and country MPs endorsed equal job opportunity, especially at times when selectors faced financial trouble. No one allowed notions of women's traditional role to get in the way, and not one of several inquiries into the postal system in the 1850s and 1860s challenged the suitability of women running post offices.[3]

The relative egalitarianism among smallholders also helps to explain the shearers' union's advanced policies on women's rights. The 'new unionism', wrote W. G. Spence, 'makes no distinction of sex.' Many union members were small selectors who also sheared part time, so:

> Spence in his appeal to country women to support the ASU also recognized each family as an economic unit, and as such insisted the support of women was crucial to the success of trade unionism.[4]

To be sure, he also took for granted many conventional notions about the female role; but so did contemporary feminists.

By the late 19th century, however, the same industrial development that was challenging the urban family was beginning to undermine these pockets of petty-bourgeois equality. The decline of craft production methods and the advent of the factory system also created routine production jobs, often filled by females and juveniles on a casual basis with high turnover levels.

REBELS IN THE WORKFORCE

Women were some 20 percent of the overall work force in late 19th century Australia, rising to 30 or 40 percent in the main urban centres. Nearly half worked in domestic service, and a sizeable proportion on farms, but that still left a large number employed in the garment and boot trades, in shops, as nurses and as teachers – though most of the jobs available, apart from domestic service, were confined to the cities and larger towns. The purely pastoral areas remained overwhelmingly male. Women's wages were one-third to one-half of men's, a difference due less to lower skill levels than to socially constructed gender roles and institutional barriers.[5] Within these broad outlines, however, the situation was steadily changing.

Census data indicate a declining number of females employed in domestic service and primary production and a moderate increase in the industrial, commercial and professional areas. Young women preferred to avoid domestic service, with its constraints on personal freedom and potential for abuse. Their search for even the worst factory work showed how much they disliked the hardships, long hours and isolation of domestic service:

> The great attractions of the factory were the company it provided at work, the sense of being one in adversity with one's fellow-sufferers, the regulated and relatively short hours, and the relatively generous pay.[6]

Outwork also proliferated in the clothing trades, suiting the domestic circumstances of some workers while allowing employers to offer piece work at low rates.

Those who still opted for domestic service were choosier. As early as 1870, when Sir George Stephens offered patronising advice to female servants, he found them unreceptive. Worse still, he was 'informed by several ladies...in search of servants that they have at times found it necessary to submit to examination themselves,' and even encountered:

> silly young women...who actually stipulated that they should be addressed as 'Miss Smith', or 'Miss Brown'... Is it possible to conceive of a more absurd request than this? For it amounts to saying, 'I am as much a lady as yourself.'[7]

Factory owners still hoped that females would be more docile than young males in this relatively tight labour market. 'Boys are far too independent,' lamented one industrialist, 'they will only take work where they like.'[8] Yet the tailoresses showed in their famous strike that the female sex might be just as rebellious as the male, because their bargaining position was steadily improving. Although the absolute number of women working rose, the 1880s still brought a relative shortage of female labour, as increasing prosperity enabled significant numbers to avoid or postpone employment just as demand was increasing.

In particular, they began to avoid domestic service, and this became a long-term trend. During the depressed 1890s, some were forced back into this type of work, and the 1901 census still showed about 10 percent of households employing servants. However, in the new century, the inexorable decline in servant numbers would continue.

In the 1870s and 1880s, more of those who became housewives could afford to hire 'help', and that increased the demand for servants. Others pursued the schooling needed to enter 'professional' jobs as teachers or public servants. The shortage of female labour pushed up women's wages: in Melbourne factories, their pay increased by half in real terms between 1871 and 1891.[9] The growth of teaching and nursing jobs created a layer of professionals with a 'respectable' status outside the home. 'The ultimate rate of payment is higher than women can make in any other employment without capital,' remarked Catherine Spence in the 1870s, 'while to most of the candidates it is a rise in the social scale; and these two considerations act powerfully enough.'[10] By 1902, 45 percent of NSW teachers and 25 percent of those in charge of schools were female. While men dominated at the top of the system, there were well over 200 Mistresses of Departments.[11] These were probably the best jobs available for women.

Nursing was also respectable in the post-Nightingale era, but the life was restrictive, the work often menial and the conditions appalling; as late as 1910, the nurses' quarters at the Royal Melbourne Hospital were known as 'Ratland'. Other possibilities included retail sales and typing. In the latter field, some women established independent businesses for a time, until the cost of typewriters fell to the point where firms could establish their own typing pools. The numbers of unmarried (and, to a lesser degree, widowed or divorced) working women were substantial enough to stimulate the growth of hostel-type accommodation, including the YWCA with its cheap, yet decent – and, above all, respectable – surroundings.

Centralisation of the public service undermined equal pay in NSW post offices after 1900. But it also created new jobs in which women could begin to assert themselves, often as part of the labour movement. In Victoria, female postal and telegraph workers had long been employed in large numbers in central locations, but at lower levels and subject to severe discrimination. This ultimately led to considerable militancy and determined organisation, and women won important concessions, including legal guarantees of equal pay.[12]

A major battle took place in the telegraph and postal unions over women's rights. The leading union journal, *The Transmitter*, supported equal pay and opportunity, as did the union in most parts of the country; but, in Victoria, male members were hostile. The main reason was mass sackings during the 1890s, which had cost 1,500 (mostly male) employees their jobs. When the Victorian Government later carried out a reclassification exercise, the local union boycotted the hearing. An ad hoc committee of women then intervened with a submission that won them improvements in salary – while males got pay cuts. The men resented this, but they should have blamed the bosses or their own tactical errors, rather than fellow workers. Women employees, for their part, were furious with those bosses whom they accused of 'unbecoming language', 'a desire to throw female assistants over the banisters' and spying on staff through holes bored in a partition.[13] Given the hostility of male unionists, they opted to form their own union.

The growth in female employment provided the material basis for both women's trade unionism and campaigns for equal rights. Having fewer children left more time and energy for organising and for politics. (Where fertility remained higher, as in Queensland, women's rights groups were weaker.) With greater access to the public sphere, more opportunities, better education and a sense of being in demand, women grew more assertive. These trends undermined the ideology relegating females to the 'private sphere'. Thousands trudged daily to the factories, with no collapse of civilisation apparent, although the more downtrodden among them aroused humanitarian concern in middle-class reformers.

Teachers and nurses proved themselves able to take on intellectually demanding tasks outside the home. It is no coincidence that such prominent champions of women's rights as Lilian Locke and Vida Goldstein both worked as teachers, or that other teachers joined the single tax leagues which supported equality. A trickle of female university graduates appeared once tertiary institutions started to become coeducational, beginning with the University of Adelaide in 1880. It was the Professor of Medicine at that university, Edward Stirling, who first introduced a motion on women's suffrage in the South Australian parliament. Stirling pointed to the success of his female students as evidence that they were men's intellectual equals.

TOWARDS WOMEN'S SUFFRAGE

Economic prosperity, which had widened women's opportunities, gave way to economic crisis in the 1890s. The experience radicalised an important minority:

> Self-supporting new middle class and working class women such as Mary Gilmore and Louisa Lawson were part of the large floating population, often from the country, who gravitated to Sydney's numerous boarding houses... Freed from family and sex role constraints, they contributed to the intellectual ferment that characterised Sydney at that time, playing an active part in the variety of 'progressive causes'... [They] were joined by women from elite families who were suddenly thrown onto the job market [and/or] radicalized by the poverty, destitution and exploitation they saw.[14]

They gathered in clubs, literary associations and suffrage leagues, although these were often fairly small and lacked influence. The common explanation is that potential activists were too busy at home with domestic tasks.[15] This explanation doesn't seem convincing; if everyone was too bogged down at home, how did they find time to get involved in the Woman's Christian Temperance Union (WCTU), which claimed thousands of members?

If they weren't up to campaigning, how do we explain their participation in the 1874 Moonta strike in South Australia, where:

> armed with brooms and led by the strike committee, the women swept those still working in the engine houses, candle factory, stables and other auxiliaries off the job.

A manager later said that they could be thankful women didn't always get involved, as 'those cousin Jennies up at Moonta showed us what can happen if they do.'[16]

The women's rights groups focusing specifically on suffrage had a modest size and impact partly because of their elite character. This was especially striking among the leading lights in NSW: Rose Scott, Lady Mary Windeyer and Dora Montefiore were all rather well off. The main issues pursued by affluent feminists, such as the vote and especially property rights, had less resonance among factory hands or working-class housewives, who were often suspicious of the prosperous ladies claiming to champion their cause - particularly in the case of proposals that limited the suffrage to property owners (and to whites).

This is why activists associated with the workers' movement sometimes kept

MEMBERS OF THE SOUTH AUSTRALIAN WORKING WOMEN'S UNION 1896

EMMA MILLER: TRADE UNION ORGANISER, SUFFRAGIST, AND KEY FIGURE IN THE FOUNDING OF THE ALP

their distance. In South Australia, Mary Lee, secretary of both the Women's Suffrage League and the Working Women's Trade Union, announced that she was not a 'women's rights woman';[17] and, in Queensland, the well-known labour activist and travelling union organiser Emma Miller led a working-class breakaway from the official suffrage organisation. In NSW, the more labour-oriented activists also split with Rose Scott in 1901.

If what we now call 'first wave feminism' was nevertheless a significant factor in late 19th century Australia, it's because of the organisational strength and continuity provided by the WCTU, which began to campaign seriously around the suffrage issue in the 1880s, hoping that women would vote to restrict alcohol. In Tasmania, it virtually *was* the movement. Only in Victoria, with its strong progressive liberal currents, and in liberal-Christian South Australia, did any significant women's rights groups form earlier than the WCTU. The temperance movement drew its members mainly from nonconformist churches, and their social background seems to have been lower-middle class. They were well organised because of the church framework and because they were supported by a previously existing male temperance movement.[18] When agitation focused on the question of national suffrage in a federated Australia, they could speak – unlike the suffrage societies – with a national voice.

Unfortunately, the WCTU was also a right-wing influence. Temperance was associated with efforts by the upper and middle classes to bring the unruly lower orders into line. In Tasmania, running the suffrage movement went hand in hand with other preoccupations:

> In 1898 the Woman's Christian Temperance Union, wanting to clear all youngsters, especially girls, off the streets at night, proposed that a curfew bell be rung at 9:00.

This was part of a general tightening up associated with the centralisation of the police force.[19] Like campaigns against prostitution, with which it was sometimes linked, the temperance crusade was a Protestant middle-class response to the growth of turbulent (heavily Irish Catholic) working-class communities in Australian cities. It had little to do with women's rights and much to do with social control.[20]

Still, the campaign for voting rights pulled together something of a women's movement across Australia. In Victoria, the WCTU took the lead in gathering a monster petition of 30,000 signatures. Among the canvassers was the young Vida Goldstein, just beginning her remarkable political career. Goldstein later commented that 'the few women who refused to sign the petition were, almost without exception, those whose interest ended at the garden gate.'[21]

This suggested that, to be more than a marginal force, the women's movement needed to get its constituency active in the public sphere. Yet, as the WCTU connection suggests, it was hampered by its own social outlook. A final reason for the small size and impact of the women's rights groups was the influence of what has been called 'domestic feminism'.

No leading figure in these circles, even Rose Scott or Vida Goldstein, who personally chose not to marry, questioned the view that woman's place was in the family sphere. Arguments for suffrage typically appealed to woman's moral role as guardian of the home, suggesting that female suffrage would help civilise society at large and claiming conversely, in Goldstein's words, that 'stability of marriage and the home depend upon our having an equal standard for men and women.'[22] Similarly, campaigners for practical dress and against tight lacing stressed the importance of women's health for their maternal role.

These arguments relied on notions that women were inherently more responsive, caring and nurturing – what Scott called the world of a 'wide, loving heart and sheltering arms'[23] – which were to find an echo in the feminism of a century later. They were also associated with moralistic campaigns for sexual puritanism, which had considerable common ground with the temperance agitation and the Salvation Army. Further, they meshed with the racist and militarist 'populate or perish' mentality of the era. This is why at least two key NSW suffrage societies publicly disowned Brettena Smyth for promoting birth control. Ordinary people flocked to hear her, but respectable suffrage ladies were appalled.

It also explains many campaigners' reluctance to support divorce reform and their emphasis on mothers' right to custody of children. 'Did she not bear them?' asked Louisa Lawson's crusading paper, *The Dawn*:

> Did she not merge her individuality into that of the helpless babe over whom she hung in its ailing weakness? It is time men acknowledged the meaning of motherhood.[24]

How this outlook limited the campaign's horizons emerges strikingly from the Queensland Women's Suffrage League's 1890 annual meeting, where Alderman J. A. Clarke suggested that there was nothing wrong with women entering parliament. His wife promptly contradicted him, declaring that the vote was quite sufficient.

The domestic feminist outlook distinguished Australian campaigners from many of their British and American sisters, who embraced a vigorous liberal philosophy emphasising individual rights. The American movement had a strong association with earlier anti-slavery agitation, while the British movement reflected the existence of a sizeable surplus of single females. By contrast, Australian marriage and fertility rates were still relatively high. The institution of marriage appeared to most people as the only realistic possibility. These social conditions gave rise to a strong family orientation which the women's rights activists could not transcend.

Of course, such views were hardly confined to feminists. On the contrary, they were the dominant social ideology, and the labour movement was also deeply imbued with them. A leader of the AWU, which supported women's rights, argued in 1889 that unionism would reduce sexual immorality by increasing wages and thereby allowing more marriages.[25] But such an outlook was particularly limiting for a movement whose success depended so specifically on getting women to look beyond the garden gate. Moreover, as the Women's Liberation Movement was to recognise many decades later, an end to female oppression depends on challenging the capitalist family, within which sexist ideas and roles are reproduced.

In the absence of such a challenge, demands for equal rights were easy to contain or coopt. Consider the case of married women's property. The issue mainly concerned the middle classes, who had property to worry about, although there was also a philanthropic concern for the poor. Introducing a reform act in the Victorian parliament, Mr J. O'Shanassy announced that its 'most prominent function' was 'the protection of the entire fabric upon which society rests', to be achieved by ensuring that wives without property and their children did not become a burden on the state.[26]

Similarly, women's suffrage went through Australian parliaments more easily than in Britain or America partly because it was promoted as a means to safeguard and elevate the existing social order, which the middle class naturally endorsed. The limited impact of this reform is evidenced by the fact that no woman sat in an Australian parliament until Edith Cowan in 1921. Betty Searle writes of Australia's middle-class suffragists:

> It was their class, and particularly its women members who most strongly promoted the ideology of motherhood and the idea of family nurturing as women's natural role which unwittingly imposed 'domestic feminist' policies on working class women... [I]n the long run women's suffrage contributed to a more orderly and stable middle class society, and helped promote legislation to benefit women and girls without upsetting the traditional sexual division of labour.[27]

GENDER AND CLASS

The family, and the social roles it cements, are a big part of holding together nation states. Australian politicians, consumed with pulling together a federation, paid a lot of attention to this around the turn of the century. So did trade unionists. One reason was that family breakdowns had become more common in the 1880s and 1890s. Pressure had grown for the liberalisation of divorce, and the birth rate had fallen. NSW government statistician Timothy Coghlan even published a pamphlet, which helped to bring on a Royal Commission on the Decline of the Birth Rate.

The semi-panic over fertility reflected the close links between family, gender issues and White Australia. Trepidation about the huge, coloured populations to the north meant that falling Australian birthrates raised the spectre of 'race suicide'. If there were not enough white people to occupy the continent, the 'yellow races' would invade it sooner or later.

On the eve of federation, a roundtable discussion in *The Worker* complained of the 'villainous wrong inflicted upon womankind by the continuance of [Melanesian] labour in our midst'.[28] Similarly, agitation against the Chinese returned again and again to their supposed designs on white females. In the labour press:

> articles dealing with the question of the Woman's Movement focussed on the Asiatics as sexual exploiters, and urged housewives to become politicised and boycott Chinese vegetable vendors.[29]

That such racism did not protect white women from abuse was demonstrated by the white Lambing Flat rioters, who showed a particular enmity towards the European wife of a Chinese: 'she was narrowly saved from being raped and her infant child from being burnt alive.'[30]

If the female role underpinned nationalism and racism, so, inevitably, did the contrasting male role – as when a politician insisted that the new nation state must be 'a federation of the manhood of Australia'.[31] South Australian MP Alexander Hill showed how this complex of ideas ran counter to female emancipation when he warned of the danger posed by women's suffrage:

> imagine a female brigade going into the House of Parliament when some great question was under discussion, such as whether we should declare war against Russia.[32]

Sexism fed on, and contributed to, the political and industrial weaknesses of organised labour. Recent work on gender and class often gives us a picture of the late 19th and early 20th centuries in which women confront a hostile, male-dominated labour movement which collaborates with the bosses and the state to exclude them from paid employment and union membership.[33] Some unions certainly did exclude them, but we have seen that, in other cases, male unionists made determined efforts to help them form unions and to back them in disputes. Still, the exclusion was inexcusable and not in the unions' long-term interest.

Why, then, did it happen? In some cases, it arose from fears that employers would use females as cheap labour to break the unions. Reporting on plans to employ female clerks in 1900, the NSW Public Service Board argued:

> No doubt the employment of women...will have the effect of curtailing to some extent the employment of men; but this will produce a result beneficial to the State, because an equal number of men will be compelled to seek positions which women cannot occupy, and therefore will be available to engage in occupations tending to develop the resources of the Colony.[34]

Here we see a direct threat to men's jobs. In other cases, the threat was not so clear. In 1889, the Typographical Society organised a boycott of Louisa Lawson's paper *The Dawn* for using female printers. On the one hand, Lawson had sacked male printers and replaced them with females – whom she paid less than union rates.[35] On the other hand, Lawson was pro-union, and it was not unusual for radical journals to pay below union rates. The boycott was based as much on sexist ideas as defence of workers' jobs or living standards. We might simply denounce male prejudice and move on, except that so many sexist ideas were embraced by the most politically aware women of the time – not only in the suffrage groups, but among female employees directly affected.

When the NSW post office dismissed married women in August 1896, there was little resistance to this by women's groups, even though one prominent female official to be retired, Lizzie Ferris, was later a member of the Womanhood Suffrage League. Even worse, 'Louisa Dunkley of the Victorian Women's Post and Telegraph Association agreed married women should resign and did so herself when she married Edward Kraegen in 1903'; and it appears that single female teachers endorsed, and even campaigned for, a ban on married women in the years before 1910.[36] Presumably, they saw the married women as unwelcome competitors.

Like racism, hostility to women's employment was linked to economic fears, but both can only be fully understood in the context of social conditions and the dominant ideas in society as a whole. These ideas relentlessly reinforced women's domestic role. A labour movement unable to defeat capitalism on the industrial or political battlefields would hardly be able to break free of its dominant ideology.

The trade unions which initially set the tone for labour fell mostly into two categories: urban craft unions, with their petty-bourgeois aspirations; and the bush unions. The craft unions were highly exclusive and tended to mimic the middle-class faith in the conventional family. Keeping women at home and out of the trade flowed naturally from this. (They also wanted to keep most males out of the trade.) If the bush unions were more sympathetic to women's rights, this flowed partly from the more egalitarian attitudes of their small farmer members, a product of the rural 'family economy'. In any case, both the exclusivism of the crafts and the rural egalitarianism of the smallholders represented social formations fated to decline; urban mass production and mass unionism were already on the rise, drawing women into production alongside men. The first signs of this, in the 1880s and 1890s, sparked labour's first serious efforts to organise women workers.

The fact that most women couldn't join unions – because of sexism, being housewives, working in non-union sweatshops, doing outwork or domestic service – didn't necessarily exclude them from the labour *movement*. They made their presence felt in a variety of labour disputes and campaigns, organising petitions and physically confronting scabs. This was noted at the time; for example, Tasmanian MP Charles Grant opposed female suffrage on the grounds that women were more emotional, as shown during strikes where 'the women, generally speaking, are the chief disturbing cause, and they hold on...for longer than men do.'[37] The conventions of the time ensured that their actions seldom made it into the historical record in this way, but that very fact suggests their role has been understated. More women are likely to have been active in the labour movement than in, say, the suffrage societies.

Female political figures conventionally viewed (through modern eyes) as 'feminists' frequently identified in some way with labour or its objectives. Vida Goldstein, for example, stood for parliament in 1903. The Labor Party was hostile to this venture, a fact commonly seen as evidence of a 'class/gender' conflict. In reality, it had more to do with the parliamentary ambitions of a political machine. The ALP rank and file, including many women, also regarded Goldstein's campaign as a threat to labour unity. They were suspicious of leading women's rights advocates who employed domestic servants, had no experience of hard work and displayed patronising attitudes towards working people.

However, we should not forget that Goldstein's election platform included such classic labour movement demands as nationalisation of coal mines, public transport and lighting. The gap between the two sides was not so immense.

The well-documented debates over female suffrage offer a precise and detailed example of the interplay between class and gender at the end of the colonial era. The new Labor Party was lukewarm about the suffrage, unless it offered clear electoral advantage. To understand why, we need to consider the social basis of the vote in 19th century Australia. There were property requirements of some kind in every colony, which ended around the turn of the century for the lower houses but remained in the upper houses. Electors with property in more than one place had more than one vote. Colonial elites claimed that property brought an insight into, or a commitment to, public affairs. Implicitly, and sometimes explicitly, the real meaning was a commitment to the existing social order.

The labour movement and progressive opinion generally, acutely aware that the upper houses had blocked popular reforms, placed great emphasis on abolishing property-based and plural voting. Conservative forces, aware that they were gradually losing ground, sought after almost any device to shore up the same practices. One of these was votes for (selected) women.

South Australia was the first colony to adopt female suffrage. However, the initial moves made in 1886 would only have given the vote to unmarried women with assets. The underlying argument, repeated in subsequent debates around the country, was that voting rights should represent property. Wives' assets were represented by their husbands' ballot, but single female property owners needed a vote of their own. South Australia had never had property-based voting for the lower house, so this was an obviously reactionary measure.

The trade unions countered with a mass petition demanding votes for all women. The conservatives tried various other

VIDA GOLDSTEIN (RIGHT) WITH WRITER MILES FRANKLIN

measures over several years, such as extending the vote just for the Upper House – sometimes stating openly that this would give the Upper House greater power, and 'if they did not take this opportunity perhaps they would not have it again'.[38]

Despite the impassioned arguments of Mary Lee, both the Suffrage League and the WCTU initially supported the bill. Then, however, the Trades and Labor Council bluntly told the League that it would only support full adult suffrage. The unions' firm stand pushed the Suffrage League to change its approach, and even the WCTU eventually recognised the manipulation behind the property vote. In other words, *it was the labour movement that took the most progressive stand.* The resulting united front between labour and the suffrage movement contributed to all South Australian women getting the vote ahead of any other colony.

The issue was posed in fairly similar terms in other colonies. In NSW, Henry Parkes impressed Rose Scott with an 1890 bill to abolish plural voting and give women the vote. The background to the bill is obscure, but Parkes' real intention was probably to preserve plural voting; he hoped that linking it to women's suffrage would reduce its appeal in sections of the parliament. Had he sincerely wished to introduce the suffrage, or to end plural voting, he could have introduced each as a separate bill.[39] In Queensland, there were many stories of squatters arranging multiple property votes through offspring and relatives.

It should now be clear that the labour movement was on solid ground opposing partial suffrage. In Queensland, labour pioneered the women's suffrage issue in the pages of William Lane's weekly *Boomerang*. Both Lane and Leontine Cooper contributed articles on the subject; Cooper also argued openly that not all women had to become wives and mothers, pointing to the large numbers who had jobs.

Labour was on weaker ground when it came to another much-debated issue of the time: whether the women's vote would be conservative. There were people on all sides of the debate who put this forward as an argument for or against. The Australian Socialist League fretted in 1891:

> if we have reason to believe that women would use voting power to keep us in our economic Slough of Despond, it is better to withhold the principle.[40]

Years later, a speaker urged the conservative Australian Women's National League to support the suffrage because its members could use their votes to oppose socialism. Then again, there were some on all sides who thought that the female vote would be left of centre.

Experience was to confirm none of these hopes or fears; as far as we can tell, women voted very much like the men of their own social background. 'To add a million women to the register is the same as to add a million men,' wrote Vida Goldstein in 1911. 'Each party gets its share.'[41] Class remained the defining feature of Australian politics.

Let there be no doubt: neither the Labor Party nor most socialists actually *opposed* women's suffrage out of fears about how they would vote. On the contrary, Labor, like most liberal politicians, was broadly on the pro-suffrage side of the argument. But in allowing this vague concern to impinge at all on an issue of principle, Labor – and especially the socialists – showed how much they were relying on votes and elections to change society. Parliamentarism and sexism went hand in hand. In the aftermath of disastrous strike defeats, and in the absence of practical experience to demonstrate how little could be expected from parliament, this was understandable. It was still mistaken, but this was a mistake shared – in inverted fashion – by the feminists, who likewise hoped that the women's vote would achieve wondrous things.

So the divisions between Labor and the suffrage groups should not be exaggerated. To some degree, they reflected justified worker suspicions of the leading women's rights figures; and, to some degree, they reflected the conservative aspects of each political current. In the case of organised labour, the conservative elements became far stronger after the defeat of the Great Strikes.

Within the labour movement, socialists stood – in principle – for women's equality. In practice, their advocacy of female emancipation was flawed, like that of the feminists, by a strong attachment to the conventional family and the division of labour that flowed from it. They might defend female workers' rights to join unions, without always understanding the importance of actively fighting to organise them.

What of the left organisations' own activities? Here, some historians have made sharp criticisms. Joy Damousi presents a damning indictment of the 'strict division of labour and the organisation of space within left-wing groups':

> The public realm of speaking, proselytising and agitating was perceived to be the preserve of male activists... women's political work was largely confined to the private, feminine and domestic space of organising fund-raising activities, such as concerts, picnics and bazaars and preparing programs and decorations for May Day celebrations.[42]

Of course, there is some factual basis for this, but the argument is completely ahistorical. Taken in the context of their time, the early Australian socialists were very advanced. The European socialist 'bible' on female emancipation, August Bebel's *Woman, Past, Present and Future*, had a considerable readership on the Australian left. So did William Lane's novel, *The Working Man's Paradise*, which challenged gender stereotypes. Lane's heroine Nelly is a union activist and the intellectual equal of the men, and she forsakes marriage for the sake of the struggle. Bruce Scates points out that both leading characters, Ned and Nelly, deviate from conventional expectations about male and female appearance and behaviour. Lane advocated equal pay and challenged the editors of the *Typographers' Journal* when that union refused women entry to the trade, writing that 'a woman has every bit as much right to work and to live as a man has'.[43]

Socialist groups debated birth control and abortion as well as that perennial favourite, 'Woman Under Socialism'. Left-wing trade unionist John Fitzgerald insisted that working women should 'be free of the meddling of male officials and come forth as the organiser of their own bodies', while his comrade Con Lindsay saw child care as a union issue. Socialist women like Rose Summerfield and Creo Stanley spoke from public platforms and tried to organise female trade unions, in the face of widespread public disapproval.

Even women's heavy involvement in the 'social' side of left activities looks different in its historical context. Virtually *all* progressive opinion accepted this division of labour at the time.

WOMEN'S BRIGADE SUPPORTING MINERS' PICKET LINE, BROKEN HILL, 1889

Moreover, the social events were more central to political life than they are today. Socialists, and the labour movement generally, relied on such activities to sustain morale and to provide an alternative to bourgeois culture. They saw the participants as making a *political* contribution; and, in a society still hostile to women intervening in public, these were ways in which:

> women traded the home for the meeting and exercised the right to speak and be heard. In this community of socialists, women claimed equal citizenship with men.[44]

5.
RACE, CLASS AND THE ROAD TO WHITE AUSTRALIA

Across northern Australia, Aboriginal and Torres Strait Islander people tell the tale of a murderous white man. He is an invader 'shooting all the people' as part of 'getting ready for the country, trying to take it away.' In his greed, violence and dishonesty this figure represents European law as seen through Black eyes.[1] The white man is Captain Cook. The saga carries a message for all of us: the violence and coercion of the state shapes any new capitalist society. Since the rise of capitalism initially benefits only a tiny minority, that minority needs the state to impose it on everyone else.

The white settlers invaded a world quite unlike their own. The Indigenous people who had dwelt in Australia for tens of thousands of years had different relationships to their physical environment and to each other. They lived in relative harmony with the land, plants and animals – which is not to say that theirs was an undifferentiated hunter-gatherer economy. Indigenous economies and settlement patterns were diverse. Population densities varied widely; while many clans lived from hunting and gathering, there were also the Dharuk, who cultivated yams along the Hawkesbury River, and along the Murray the Yorta Yorta and others:

> had developed such sustained harvesting of the rich fish, game and plants that they lived virtually sedentary lives in villages which were observed by the earliest white explorers.

Grassland clans used firestick farming and, on the Darling River:

> engineering works like the extensive Brewarrina fisheries were constructed to maintain a consistent yield of fish no matter how dry or flooded the rivers might be.[2]

While the popular prejudice that Indigenous people 'did nothing with the land' was nonsense, the social context was very different. Association with the land appears to have been more a matter of key sites than the sharp boundaries that white property-owners enforced. Whites wrongly took this to imply that there was no fixed relationship at all. In reality, social relations were expressed through relations to land, while knowledge and tradition were closely linked to location. Work was also different. Indigenous people often worked until they had enough for their immediate needs, then turned to ritual or social activities that they considered just as useful. The capitalist imperative to work and to accumulate wealth, as ends in themselves, weren't at the centre of Indigenous culture.

Social organisation was relatively egalitarian, and class divisions were unheard of. The idea of some people dominating and exploiting others struck them as tragic when they encountered it among whites. A Victorian clergyman complained that it was 'difficult to get into a black-fellow's head that one man is higher than another'.[3]

Each clan had its territory. Clashes might occur at the margins, but territorial conquest was virtually unknown, because the clans' ties to specific territories were not conceived in terms of 'ownership' or capital accumulation. They had well-defined clan identities but no notion of nationality or race. Initially, they tended to regard the Europeans as people like themselves who had developed curious customs and acquired an odd skin colour. They often tried to fit the whites into their kinship systems and didn't, at first, see the conflict with white colonists in racial terms. Whites were treated as just another clan, or set of clans. Only after massacres by the invaders did they begin to see the conflict as one between all whites and all Blacks, concluding 'that white people were mutually accountable for each other's actions and therefore fit subjects for Aboriginal attack. Colour alone was now enough to identify the enemy.'[4]

Almost immediately, the new arrivals sowed the seeds of conflict over control and use of the land and natural environment. The First Fleet had brought only limited supplies, so the colonists had to exploit the surrounding landscape; they found that 'the natives were well pleased with our People until they began clearing the Ground at which they were displeased' and that some Indigenous people were enraged at the sight of convicts cutting down trees.[5] The Indigenous people themselves sometimes cut down trees – for example, to make canoes. But they had noticed the whites doing something quite different and seemingly irrational: piling up logs and stones, clearing large tracts, erecting unwieldy structures. It was their first experience of the drive to accumulate wealth that was to transform the continent.

Until the 1820s, the white settlements at Sydney and Hobart were tiny. However, the rapid growth of a capitalist economy after 1820 began to transform a localised, erratic conflict into a genocidal '100 years' war'. Systematic warfare against the Indigenous people was driven by British industry's insatiable demand for wool and the local settlers' hunger for land so that the pastoral industry could supply that wool.

Sheep numbers in Van Diemen's Land were around 436,000 in 1827, rising to 680,000 three years later and approaching 1,000,000 by 1836.[6] There was no room for Indigenous people in this new capitalist landscape; they experienced at first hand a fundamental and brutal truth of the age, that 'what happened to land determined the life and death of most human beings in the years 1789 to 1848.' Odd as it sounds, the Indigenous people had something in common with Celtic clans forced off communal lands in the Scottish Highlands to make way for capitalist sheep runs, after which Celtic bards lamented that 'nothing was heard but the bleating of sheep and the voices of English speakers'.[7]

After the 1988 Bicentenary celebrations, a debate raged over whether to call the founding of NSW 'settlement' or 'invasion'. Of course, it was an invasion; what else do you call seizing someone's country by force? But there is also an organic link between the two aspects. Settlement necessarily meant the violent destruction of traditional Aboriginal society, precisely because the conflict was more than a race war. It was also a *conflict between two incompatible modes of production* and the cultures that accompanied them. Capitalism could not flourish without crushing the resistance of people who wanted to live differently, in every corner of the globe. Private property, wage labour and the drive to accumulate capital were incompatible with Aboriginal society.

Many Indigenous people fought back strongly across much of the frontier. I offer two examples. A warrior from the NSW Hawkesbury region, named Musquito, was exiled to Tasmania and ultimately led a band of Tasmanian Indigenous people in many skilfully planned and targeted raids against the whites before being captured and executed; so skilfully planned were his raids that arrogant Europeans 'insisted they were being led by a white man.'[8] Another leader, Tarenorerer of the Emu Bay tribe, called Walyer by the whites, 'was said to stand on a hill and give

INDIGENOUS PEOPLE'S CAMP, SOUTH AUSTRALIA, 1879

orders to the Aborigines'[9] who were attacking the hated whites. Banished to Penguin Island, she tried to kill her captors en route. Finally, she was sent to the 'Friendly Mission' on Swan Island, where she again tried to organise a revolt and was captured. She died of influenza while in captivity.

There were many other cases. When Thomas Mitchell was exploring northern NSW in the 1840s, he wrote of one district where 'humiliating proofs that the white man had given way were visible in the remains of dairies burnt down, stockyards in ruins, untrodden roads'.[10]

No amount of cleverness or courage could stem the European onslaught. But, although defeat was inevitable, Indigenous resistance was by no means futile. The Indigenous people held enough ground to force the British authorities to take notice.

WORKERS AT DURUNDUR STATION, QUEENSLAND, 1867:
NUDLA, MICKY, TUNDARUN, WEERUM, KING BUCKNER, NICKER, NANCY, MARIA, LUCY

After the ending of slavery in the 1830s, humanitarians in the home country were turning their attention to Indigenous people in the colonies, just as reports about massacres of Australian Indigenous people reached London. Under British pressure, colonial governments began to intervene. NSW established a Protectorate for Aborigines, with Indigenous land and cultural interests and hunting practice being recognised for the first time. These measures were limited, paternalistic and oppressive in many ways, but significant as a partial recognition of what today we know as Land Rights.

The Aboriginal and Torres Strait Islander clans resisted white settlement for the sake of sheer survival; in an attempt to maintain their traditional relationship with the land; and out of hostility to the oppressive and exploitative aspects of the invading society. This hostility was sometimes quite explicit. In 1843, two Indigenous people intent on attacking a sheep station:

approached a hutkeeper near Glendon and asked for the property owner. When told he was mustering sheep in another part of his property, they then enquired if the hutkeeper was a convict or a free settler. The hutkeeper replied that he was a former convict. He was then told by the [Indigenous people] that it was fortunate for him, because he was forced to come to their lands and was not like the free settler who came and took over the land and gave the [Indigenous people] nothing in return.[11]

Similarly, a pioneer squatter told in 1861 of a case where Blacks killed a bullock, then:

advanced on the hut of the beleaguered squatter with the animal's kidney fat stuck on their spears. They called out to the whites offering them a share of the fat, saying 'that they were not like the whites themselves – greedy.'[12]

Because Indigenous people traditionally shared the fruits of their labour, they rejected the European approach to private property. The differences were especially great when it came to the land, which the Indigenous people did not see themselves as 'owning' in the capitalist sense. 'Their system of socialism', lamented a Queensland clergyman, hindered 'any improvement or rightful ownership.'[13] Similarly, if individual workers were paid more for greater efficiency, they immediately shared the payment with kin.

Because they didn't think in terms of accumulating wealth, Indigenous people didn't live by the capitalist 'work ethic'. A plantation owner who used Indigenous labour complained that there was 'no means by which I could persuade them into sudden acceptance of a daily routine of toil'. In Western Australia, Governor Hutt thought Indigenous attitudes to labour were the 'chief and serious difficulty' preventing assimilation.[14] It was partly in an attempt to socialise their children into 'a habit of labour' that schemes were hatched that separated generations of Indigenous children from their parents.[15]

After the gold rushes, with the increased small farming population in many areas of southeastern Australia, there was antagonism between white farmers and Indigenous people over access to schools and other local services, which sharpened in the 1890s depression and the following drought. Governments responded to this by forcing more Indigenous people into reserves. In some cases, whites tried to usurp Aboriginal holdings; the authorities stopped them, but imposed greater control over the Blacks. At Kinchela, NSW, whites challenged Indigenous control of fertile land in 1899. The Protection Board stepped in to secure the Indigenous people's continued residency, but at the price of transforming the land into a reserve. This placated racist smallholders, but the real benefits went to the employers of Black labour; they advised the Board about where reserves should be located to make the best uses of labour. Once again, the dynamics of capitalism lurked within the conflict between races.

HOW WHITE AUSTRALIA TOOK SHAPE

Australian racism and ethnic hatreds developed from many sources. One important starting point was the ideology of the imperialist frontier, which sought to justify the subjugation of 'inferior' races and flowered along with the war on Indigenous people and expansion in the Pacific. This mentality raises its head today, when the Australian Government tells us that Pacific Island nations can't run their own affairs.

Another strand was hostility to the (predominantly Catholic and working class) Irish. After an Irishman shot Prince Alfred at Clontarf (near Sydney) in 1868, there was a major (middle-class) Protestant mobilisation; on one estimate, the Orange Lodges enrolled 15 percent of the adult male Protestants of NSW.[16] This sectarian push was associated with middle-class 'wowser' campaigns against drink, prostitution and all forms of 'vice', running parallel to campaigns against the opium, disease and sexual degradation supposedly associated with the Chinese.

There was also a highly ambiguous linkage to the struggle against the convict system and transportation of convicts. On the one hand, this struggle had its progressive side; the semi-slave nature of convict labour was a threat to workers' struggles and organisations, and opposing convictism was associated with the campaign for democracy. Conversely, the continuing existence of the convict system was used against the democratic movements. The anti-democratic elements in the British and colonial elites insisted that a prison couldn't be a democracy, and demands for self-government and widening the suffrage often came up against the response that a society full of criminals wasn't fit to rule itself. On the other hand, aspects of the argument against 'cheap labour' being brought in from outside could be readily transferred to campaigns against non-white immigrants such as Asians and Pacific Islanders.

Yet another strand, of course, was the 'yellow peril' fears, centred initially on Chinese immigrants but later also on Japan as an emerging force in the Pacific. We'll consider anti-Chinese paranoia in some detail below.

These strands intersected in many ways. They had a common ideological starting point in British imperialism, which was associated with colonisation and the slave trade and gave rise to doctrines of white supremacy. The 'moral' campaigns against Irish workers and the Chinese both embodied an attempt to control women's sexuality and to bolster the (white, middle-class, Protestant) family. Even so, they were only loosely connected. For example: 'Few documents...link contemporary perceptions of Aborigines and Chinese. When anti-Chinese agitators looked for relevant examples from history, they cited the anti-transportation movement'.[17] Anti-Irish prejudice was clearly not about skin colour at all, being in many ways a reflection of class antagonism.

Racist ideology cohered in the latter half of the 19th century with the rise of 'social Darwinism', which gave white domination the gloss of evolutionary progress. Australian scholars produced histories that either trivialised or ignored the struggles and claims of Indigenous people. Then, in 1889, the Privy Council laid down the principle that all of Australia had become crown land, because the country was *terra nullius*, meaning 'practically unoccupied, without settled inhabitants or settled law'.[18]

In the first part of the century, fears of Asian immigrants had been just one issue among many, generally overshadowed by agitation against transportation. By the late 19th century, fear of the 'yellow peril' was well on its way to becoming a defining theme of Australian nationalism and a pillar of the nation state arising out of federation.

The conventional view is that 19th century racist agitation, and especially demands to exclude Chinese, were driven by the common people. The labour movement, in particular, is supposed to have forced the ruling circles to exclude Chinese from the country. On this account, White Australia (like the exclusion of women from many jobs) appears to stem from the power of organised, white, male labour. But that version of history raises some important questions.

Why and how should the workers' movement, which proved unable to impose its will in the strike battles of the 1890s, have achieved this one political victory? That is never satisfactorily explained. Why the bourgeoisie, which fought bitterly to impose 'freedom of contract' in the industrial sphere, should have legislated to protect workers from Chinese competition is likewise unclear. Moreover, this whole line of argument ignores the central role of racism in the British Empire well before Australian trade unions became a force. The slave trade; genocide against Indigenous peoples; colonial wars on several continents; all preceded Australian campaigns for White Australia. Verity

Burgmann, who makes these points, reminds us that the dominant ideas in capitalist society are generally those of the ruling class. So it was with colonial racism.[19]

Phil Griffiths has pointed out in an important study that the anti-Chinese legislation passed in colonial Australia was the product of parliaments whose membership was not paid, which meant that they were all from affluent backgrounds; these were *elite institutions* in the most literal sense. Griffiths goes on to explain why the bourgeoisie opted for White Australia.[20]

Firstly, they feared that, should a large Chinese population settle in the north, it might be hard to control and even become a beachhead for invasion. Moreover, it might begin to move south. The fear of invasion was a constant feature of late 19th century Australian politics.

Secondly, they worried that the importation of a large non-white population might be associated with the development of a plantation economy in parts of the continent. They disliked this prospect, not out of anti-racism but because it represented a rival form of economic and social development. In the USA, conflict between the slave-based system of plantation agriculture and the northern industrial economy based on wage labour had led to a civil war. British Empire critics believed that US slavery had also given rise to a class of troublesome 'poor whites'. Consequently, the dominant view in both Australian and British ruling circles was that Australasia should remain a (white) British domain. James Stephen of the Colonial Office wrote:

> As we now regret the folly of our ancestors in colonising North American from Africa, so should our posterity have to censure us if we should colonise Australia from India.[21]

Like the genocidal war on the Indigenous people, the White Australia policy can't be understood apart from the peculiar features of the capitalist mode of production and the imperialist framework of settlement.

Thirdly, White Australia was a convenient ideology for convincing white workers that they had common interests with the white ruling class. This became increasingly important as the unions grew stronger and capitalists began to fear a generalised challenge to their power. Racist agitation could help forestall such a threat.

The great urban working-class mobilisations against Chinese immigration all came at times of unemployment and economic distress: 1878 in NSW and elsewhere, 1880 in NSW, and 1888 in Sydney, Melbourne and Brisbane. Bitterness at the workings of capitalism was deflected – deliberately or otherwise – onto a racialised target.[22]

When we look closely at race riots and the climate that generates them, we tend to find local merchants and politicians setting the tone, sometimes taking their cue from British imperialism. In his suitably titled newspaper, *The Empire*, Henry Parkes wrote in 1851 that importing 'coloured races' was 'an act of treason to society'.[23] During the 1862 Lambing Flat riots in NSW, Charles Allen, a prominent local shopkeeper, chaired the meeting that resolved to drive out the Chinese. In Victoria, as Jerome Small points out: 'The first recorded voice raised against the Chinese was...William Westgarth, founder of the Melbourne Chamber of Commerce in 1853.' A few years later, just prior to the 1857 Buckland riots, the colony's Legislative Council established a committee led by landowner John Pascoe Fawkner to keep 'the hordes of Asia' away from the goldfields. Restrictions imposed by governments, designed to keep the races apart both in their work and in residential areas, themselves contributed to the fears and ignorance from which racism sprang.[24] In the 1878 seamen's strike discussed in Chapter 2, it was a politician, Angus Cameron, who opened the racist campaign.

These facts help to explain why Sydney's mayor could lead a rowdy demonstration against Chinese arrivals; why the Brisbane *Courier* reported that local race riots in 1888 had been 'at least

CHINESE WORKERS BEING SEARCHED BY CUSTOMS OFFICIALS, VICTORIA, 1895

encouraged by persons whose social position should have placed them above such behaviour';[25] and why the community mobilisation associated with the 1878 seamen's strike was strongest in Queensland – where it was not the unions, but prominent MPs who took the lead.

Where competition *was* a factor, it didn't primarily affect wage earners. Mass agitation against the Chinese was common on the goldfields, where *self-employed diggers*, often in economic dire straits, carried out most of the violence. The riots at Buckland and elsewhere in 1857–58, the height of the first round of anti-Chinese agitation in Victoria, came at a time of declining returns.

Similarly:

> by the time of the Lambing Flat riots in 1860–61, thousands of white diggers had come to see that series of gold strikes as a final chance to achieve wealth or to recover the investment of a life's savings.

They would go to extreme lengths to stop the Chinese getting in ahead of them.[26]

In addition to the petty bourgeoisie, some big capitalists faced competitive pressures. In Melbourne, local industrialists became alarmed in 1880, when a Chinese rival tendered successfully to build 500 dozen chairs for the Exhibition Building.

> Furthermore, the Colonial Sugar Refining Company was keen to exclude Indian labour as well as Indian capital, since cheap labour enabled smaller concerns to survive... Likewise, the 'lumpen petty bourgeoisie' of Indian, Afghan or Syrian hawkers was resented by white merchants. In 1896 the Victorian government, responding to requests by the Country Traders' Association of Victoria, passed legislation refusing hawking licenses to coloured immigrants.[27]

Selectors (small farmers) were close to the frontier and the ongoing war against Indigenous people; in more settled areas, they fought with them over access to services in the towns and tried to encroach on fringe land the Indigenous people had occupied. We have seen examples of clashes between farmers and Indigenous people in NSW. Similarly, in the northern NSW sugar industry, it was farmers and a local newspaper editor, not workers, who took the lead in organising agitation against non-white labour.[28]

It is true that wage earners felt similar fears, but it's interesting to consider which ones were most alarmed: it was wage-earning *miners* – precisely because of the petty-bourgeois environment that surrounded them. A good example is the 1873 Clunes upheaval, in which miners rioted against Chinese who were being used as scabs. We would tend to see this as a workers' action; on closer examination, we find that the Clunes Miners' Association which fought the Chinese counted local businessmen among its members. We also find that in Ballarat East, the one area where Chinese and white workers had been permitted to live side by side, the miners were less racist, and the local Chinese did not scab on them.[29]

While conscious anti-racism among whites was unusual, it was not unheard of. Initially, tolerance for the Chinese was common enough. The first major anti-Chinese agitation on the Bendigo goldfields, in 1854, saw only a narrow majority call for restricted immigration. At Castlemaine, a spokesman told the *Argus* that the diggers had no feeling against the Chinese, adding: 'Englishmen are ever ready to receive foreigners as brethren with open arms.'[30] Such tolerance faded; yet elements of it remained. Among the worst goldfields riots, there were always some whites who were appalled at the racial violence. There were also cases of white diggers accepting African Americans. The most dramatic example was Joseph, an African American miner from New York, whom the authorities prosecuted first in the trials after the Eureka Stockade, presumably hoping to play on racism. 'The jury found Joseph not guilty and he was greeted as a hero by hundreds of supporters outside the Supreme Court.'[31]

The non-whites themselves were by no means willing to be passive victims of persecution. In Victoria, 'Chinese showed themselves willing to resist European mobs when they held a marked superiority in numbers and in several cases expelled Europeans from gold fields'. After the Buckland riot, Chinese were 'almost universally armed and could be seen exercising in military formation.'[32] When the government imposed special taxes on them, the majority refused to pay, responding with protest meetings of thousands. In May 1859 in Bendigo, they fought police in an attempt to free arrested Chinese miners and, when this failed, hundreds demanded to be arrested in a mass

SOUTH SEA ISLANDER WOMEN SUGAR CANE LABOURERS, QUEENSLAND 1895

civil disobedience campaign. In Castlemaine, some 3,000 made similar demands. Later, in the pastoral industry, Chinese staged a number of strikes. At Canning Downs, they took up shear blades to use as daggers and locked themselves in the wool store; at Pikedale, they marched to the homestead to complain about their wages.

Other non-whites were not the meek and anti-union types that white racists imagined. In 1846, an employer at Tent Hill, NSW, complained that his 25 Indian labourers had been satisfied with their lot 'until they were tampered with', whereupon they demanded European rations.[33] In Bourke in 1899, the Afghans employed as camel drivers struck for higher wages and were imprisoned. Melanesians, too, began striking to push up wages, despite conditions not far from slavery – there were actual auctions of Islanders in the 1870s and one case of branding. Despite this oppression, their ability to win higher pay became a factor in the eventual demise of the plantation system.

Tragically, however, white unionists remained indifferent. One industry with numerous Asian workers was the furniture trades, where:

> in 1885 the Chinese cabinetmakers fought a successful battle for higher wages and formed a union which enforced minimum rates of pay and a fifty hour week... But the Europeans contemptuously ignored these efforts... Indeed, when Chinese workers donated to a fund to aid striking shearers, the European cabinetmakers indignantly demanded that the donations...be refused. During a strike by Chinese early in 1893, prominent trade unionists chose to avert their eyes, a leader of the Trades Hall Council remarking: 'We can afford to laugh. It does not affect us.'[34]

WORKING CLASS RACISM AND THE CONSOLIDATION OF WHITE AUSTRALIA

While mass racism did not emerge with, or emanate from, organised labour, it is certainly true that workers embraced it. The conventional explanation is that they felt threatened by competition from coloured labour. Let's consider this more closely.

Few white workers competed directly with non-whites. For those who did:

> where evidence is available, Chinese workers' wages were on a par with Europeans, although they were often paid by the piece, a practice the unions strongly objected to.[35]

On any logical measure, assisted migration from the British Isles should have seemed a greater threat to the interests of white workers than Chinese or Islander labour; the numbers were

HENRY PARKES ELECTION POSTER, 1890s (CROPPED)

larger, and assisted white labour was more readily manipulated. Chinese labour was usually confined to certain sectors (such as the furnishing trades) and to Chinese employers, while Islanders were confined to tropical zones and plantation work. On purely economic grounds, they couldn't be portrayed as much of a threat outside the North Queensland sugar industry.

Even for the canefields, the competition argument doesn't withstand serious scrutiny. White workers preferred mining or pastoral work and showed little enthusiasm for the canefields:

> In 1901 the state government labour bureau agent at Gin Gin complained that despite a demand for cane cutters, unemployed European labourers had shown no interest ... [and] that at one mill in the Cairns district, "409 white labourers passed through the books in order to provide and maintain a daily requirement of 88 hands".[36]

Only during the 1890s depression were whites keen to take on these jobs. This had something to do with the stigma of 'kanakas' work' but also much to do with miserable pay and conditions. While white workers undoubtedly opposed the use of Islander labour, they seldom mobilised around the question; it was largely seen as an electoral issue best left to Labor politicians.

It's quite true that workers *perceived* non-whites as competitors. Such anxieties accompany all opposition to immigration, and given the assumption of white supremacy, fears about non-white labour followed inexorably.

These apprehensions could be quite intense, and might even become self-fulfilling, since racism itself made it easier for employers to play off one group against another. But generally they weren't rational, and neither were they the starting point for White Australia. Economic, social, political and ideological factors formed a complex pattern that we can't reduce to competition for jobs. If we want to emphasize one factor, it makes more sense to consider class collaboration. Workers and their unions, not confident enough to fight battles on their own, embraced racism as part of class alliances that linked them to the bosses and to society's middle layers. Thus like sexism, racial prejudice actually reflected the *weaknesses* of the labour movement rather than its strengths.

The working class was not concentrated in mass production, nor even entirely in the cities. Some sections, such as the shearers, included a large proportion of people who were really small proprietors. Another large element, especially craftsmen and their families, dreamed of petty-bourgeois independence from wage labour. Socialist ideas were confused, and the left within the labour movement was relatively weak. Under such conditions, the temptation to build unions and industrial campaigns around issues that linked the unions to middle-class elements and to the employers was strong. Race was just such an issue, precisely because important sections of the employers and small business had their own reasons to exclude Chinese and other non-Europeans. Protectionism and the family wage were other issues with similar implications.

Meanwhile, the upper classes sometimes used the race issue quite blatantly to distract workers from the task of fighting the boss. In 1886, a miners' union had no sooner formed at Charters Towers than the local newspaper editor pressed for its conversion into 'a union of all classes against the common enemy, John Chinaman.'[37]

Employers inflamed the race question during industrial disputes. In Victoria's quartz mines, the unions certainly used anti-Chinese agitation to recruit members and fought to exclude them from the mines. However, the employers also tried to use Chinese as strikebreakers during a long dispute over the eight-hour day. The strikers and their wives drove the strikebreakers away with a hail of stones. We shouldn't make excuses for racism. Of course, the unionists should have accepted the Chinese and recruited them to the union, so that they couldn't be used to break strikes. On the other hand, the bosses were hardly innocent in the affair.

Sometimes, the unions resisted racism better than other groups. Selectors who travelled the wool track were often ferociously anti-Aboriginal, and this made the AWU a centre of racism. At the same time, the shearers' paper, *The Hummer*, exposed the dreadful conditions facing Aboriginal pastoral workers, and the union didn't exclude them from its ranks. The ASU's 1891 conference voted to admit them for half the normal fee, with some delegates describing Indigenous workers as better unionists than whites.[38] In 1889, Robert Stevenson, a militant shearers' leader, convinced the union's Bourke branch to allow Chinese to retain membership. 'The Bourke members, predominantly landless labourers, were more open to ideas of working class unity than members nearer the coast where small farmers predominated.'[39]

Nevertheless, by the turn of the century, white supremacy had become an essential plank of the national ideology in every sphere. It was advanced to justify the conquest of the land and the exploitation of Indigenous labour in the pastoral industry and had provided a rationale for expansion in the Pacific and the exploitation of Pacific Islander labour in the Islands as well as on Queensland plantations. Meanwhile, in the mainstream of domestic politics, where racism could be used to tie workers to the employers and the state, the same white supremacy meant the *exclusion* of coloured labour. This helps explain why, in Alfred Deakin's eyes, the strongest argument for federation was 'the desire that we should be one people, and remain one people, without the admixture of other races'.[40]

Racism was *essential* to cement federation. It wasn't easy creating a capitalist nation state across the Australian continent. The colonial population lacked a strong sense of national identity. What did they all have in common, especially after the bitter class divisions of the 1890s? The new state was highly federal, and Barton's first cabinet had to contain someone from every state because centrifugal pressures were so strong. However, the government's first major legislation in 1901 pushed the country towards greater centralisation: the *Immigration Restriction Act* and the *Pacific Island Labourers Act*:

> brought in their wake a whole series of administrative problems, involving such diverse matters as the dictation test and the payment of bounties to sugar-growers who employed only white labour. The solution of these problems marked a much more rapid assertion of Commonwealth authority than most people had expected, and the exercise of that authority cut sharply across conflicting state interests. Within a very short time a significant number of people in all the colonies, but most particularly in New South Wales, began to wonder whether they had not been victims of a confidence trick.[41]

Barton got away with it because his measures touched the one nerve that could arouse and unite most of the population: White Australia. That ideology also underpinned the now well-established Australian imperialism, and both intersected with another pillar of the new state: conventional gender roles and the nuclear family. The male ideal was captured in a virile image of the Australian 'Coming Man'; beside him stood an image of the ideal white woman as the lynchpin of family life, reproducer of the race, guardian of its purity. British and Australian colonists took the latter issue very seriously, particularly on the frontier and in places like Fiji:

> where the maintenance of minority power and status was seen to depend on racial purity [and] where the white woman was unquestionably the protector of the white home.[42]

In such situations, European women were under great pressure to bear lots of children, and their ability to work was particularly limited, because it would undermine white prestige if they engaged in physical labour.

Sexual morality was also particularly stifling for white females. They were expected to provide a sharp contrast to 'native' women, who were portrayed as morally lax.

Even seemingly progressive movements were all too readily poisoned by racism. Opposition to the Pacific labour trade arose partly from racist hostility to the introduction of Pacific Islander labour into Australia, while opposition to the Boer War arose from sympathy with another group of white settlers colonising the land of non-whites. *The Worker* blamed the Boer War on 'a plot of the Jew capitalists', and Henry Lawson warned Australian troops about 'niggers' crawling into their tents at night to 'rip out your innards'.[43] Indeed, there was a strong white supremacist streak in arguments both for and against the war:

> Pro-Boers felt that that most cherished ideal [White Australia] was violated by a war which was engineered by financial interests to secure an assured supply of cheap labour for the mines – black, brown, yellow or depressed white.... Supporters of the war simply dismissed this interpretation and construed their own support as a premium to insure the inviolability of White Australia.[44]

Because most critics of imperialism shared the nationalist and racist sentiments, it was easier for them to eventually embrace the imperialist logic. Although Henry Lawson had claims to being a socialist supporter of class struggles and had sympathised with the enemy during the Boer War, the defeat of those struggles in the 1890s pushed him in a reactionary direction. By 1905, he was supporting the British presence in India and hailing Russia as the champion of the white races in 'the struggle of the East against the West'.[45]

The Labor Party was an important part of consolidating White Australia, but not in quite the way this is usually understood. The standard view is that Labor's racism reflected the views of its worker supporters, which it sought to champion in parliament. Of course, this is part of the story; but the great appeal of racism for the ALP was precisely that it *appealed to all classes*, including the party's small farmer voting base. In Labor's political program, racism and the land issue connected with a specifically Australian (as opposed to British) republican nationalism whose greatest appeal in the 1890s appears to have been in the bush, rather than in the cities. Among unionists, it was the AWU that rallied most conspicuously to the Eureka flag. Whereas the capitalist parties were generally British Empire patriots, Labor could appeal to the Australian and the Irish-born from different social layers on the basis of an apparently anti-imperialist stance, inseparable from racism because it incorporated demands for more aggressive expansionism in the Pacific than London would contemplate – there were complaints that Britain was selling out the white race in the Pacific.[46]

The Labor Party also displayed other, more progressive tendencies associated with its militant, urban working-class supporters, but these supporters were weakened by industrial defeat in the maritime strike and by mass unemployment in the subsequent depression.[47] The taming of the ALP through racism was part of what is sometimes called the 'National Settlement' underpinning the new Australian state after federation. It reflected, and often reinforced, the weaknesses of organised labour more than its strengths. Just as the new state was built on the oppression of women and non-whites, so it was also built on labour's failures in the 1890s.

That state remains today, its oppressive nature changed in form but not in essence. Yet the traditions of resistance also remain, with lessons to guide us in today's struggles. Because history is usually written by the victors, all too often the traditions get obscured. I hope that this book has cast more light on them.

ENDNOTES

PREFACE

1. T. Irving, *The Southern Tree of Liberty*, Sydney, Federation Press, 2006.
2. B. Fitzpatrick, *A Short History of the Australian Labor Movement*, Melbourne, MacMillan, 1968.
3. E. Hobsbawm, *The Forward March of Labour Halted?*, London, Verso, 1981.
4. M. Quinlan, *The Origins of Worker Mobilisation: Australia 1788–1850*, New York, Routledge, 2017.
5. M. Quinlan, *Contesting Inequality and Worker Mobilisation: Australia 1851–1880*, New York, Routledge, 2020.
6. T. Irving, Review of Michael Quinlan, *The Origins of Worker Mobilisation: Australia 1788–1850*, in *The Economic and Labour Relations Review*, 2018, 29(2), pp. 263–268.

INTRODUCTION

1. I. Turner, *Room for Manoeuvre: Writings on History, Politics, Ideas and Play*, Richmond, Drummond Publishing, 1982, p. 16.
2. Fitzpatrick, *A Short History of the Australian Labor Movement*, p. 63.

CHAPTER 1

1 An earlier version of Chapter 1 appeared in *Reconstruction*, no. 7, Autumn 1996. Verity Burgmann thought of the title, which is a line from a song, 'The Red Flag'.

2 L. Thomas, *The Development of the Labour Movement in the Sydney District of New South Wales*, MA Thesis, Sydney University 1919, reprinted by the Australian Society for Labour History, Canberra, 1962, p. 5.

3 F.K. Crowley, *Working Class Conditions in Australia, 1788–1851*, Ph.D. Thesis, Melbourne Unversity, 1949, pp. 101–2.

4 Quoted in Crowley, *Working Class Conditions in Australia*, p. 364.

5 Crowley, *Working Class Conditions in Australia*, p. 349.

6 Crowley, *Working Class Conditions in Australia*, p. 486.

7 Quoted in Crowley, *Working Class Conditions in Australia*, p. 487.

8 Quoted in Crowley, *Working Class Conditions in Australia*, p. 308.

9 First and third quotes: *Port Phillip Gazette*, 14 May 1845. Second quote: *The Star & Working Man's Guardian*, 31 May 1845.

10 *Sydney Morning Herald*, 15 June 1837.

11 J. Baker, *Communicators and their First Trade Unions: A History of the Telegraphist and Postal Clerk Unions of Australia*, Sydney, Union of Postal Clerks and Telegraphists, 1980, p. 42.

12 All quotes on the currency strike are taken from Thomas, *The Development of the Labour Movement*, pp. 27–8, except the *Australian* editorial, which appeared 1 December 1829.

13 'P.P. Bakers', *Record*, Melbourne Branch, Australian Society for the Study of Labour History, No 52, June 1971.

14 See M. Quinlan and M. Gardner, 'Strikes, Worker Protest and Union Growth in Canada and Australia, 1815–1900: a Comparative Analysis of Available Data', *Labour/Le Travail*, St John, Newfoundland, Canada, no. 36, Autumn 1995.

15 Quote taken from Thomas, *The Development of the Labour Movement in the Sydney District*, p. 29, followed by her own words, p. 30.

16 Quotes and details from Thomas, *The Development of the Labour Movement in the Sydney District*, pp. 40–41.

17 Details on NSW from L.J. Hume, 'Working Class Movements in Sydney

and Melbourne Before the Gold Rushes', *Historical Studies*, vol. 9, no. 35, November 1960; details on South Australia from M. Quinlan, 'Early Trade Union Organisation in Australia: Three Colonies, 1829–50', *Labour and Industry*, vol. 1, no. 11, October 1987.

18 J. Moss, *Sound of Trumpets: History of the Labour Movement in South Australia*, Adelaide, Wakefield Press, 1985, p. 25.

19 For a detailed discussion of the strike, see M. Davies, 'Cornish Miners and Class Relations in Early Colonial South Australia: The Burra Burra Strikes of 1848–49', *Australian Historical Studies*, vol. 26, no. 105, October 1995.

20 Quoted in Quinlan, 'Early Trade Union Organisation', pp. 71–2.

21 Shown by a graph attached to Crowley, *Working Class Conditions in Australia*.

22 Quotes taken from D.H.M. Terry, *The Development of the Labour Movement in New South Wales 1833–1846*, MA Thesis, Sydney University, 1951, p. 61.

23 Quotes from Terry, *The Development of the Labour Movement*, pp. 71–4.

24 Quotes taken from Terry, *The Development of the Labour Movement*, pp. 77, 87.

25 Thomas, *The Development of the Labour Movement in the Sydney District*, p. 19.

26 Thomas, *The Development of the Labour Movement in the Sydney District*, p. 22.

27 Terry, *The Development of the Labour Movement*, p. 148.

28 Quoted in Terry, *The Development of the Labour Movement*, p. 149.

29 Both quotes taken from Thomas, *The Development of the Labour Movement in the Sydney District*, p. 66.

30 Quoted in V. Burgmann, 'Capital and Labour', in A. Curthoys and A. Markus (eds.), *Who Are Our Enemies? Racism and the Working Class in Australia*, Sydney, Hale and Iremonger, 1978, p. 25.

31 Quoted in Terry, *The Development of the Labour Movement*, p. 113.

32 Quoted in Terry, *The Development of the Labour Movement*, p. 113.

33 Quoted in Thomas, *The Development of the Labour Movement in the Sydney District*, p. 78.

34 Quinlan, 'Early Trade Union Organisation', p. 65.

35 Quinlan, 'Early Trade Union Organisation', p. 81.

36 Quinlan, 'Early Trade Union Organisation', p. 84.

37 Quinlan, 'Early Trade Union Organisation', p. 85.

38 Quoted in Quinlan, 'Early Trade Union Organisation', p. 87.

CHAPTER 2

1   G. Patmore, *Australian Labour History*, Melbourne, Longman Cheshire, 1991, p. 58.

2   Quoted in H. Hughes, 'The Eight Hour Day and the Development of the Labour in Victoria in the Eighteen-Fifties', *Historical Studies*, vol. 9, no. 36, 1961.

3   Hughes, 'The Eight Hour Day', p. 399

4   Hughes, 'The Eight Hour Day', p. 405

5   E. Ross, *A History of the Miners' Federation of Australia*, Sydney, Australasian Coal and Shale Employees' Federation, 1970, p. 18.

6   Ross, *A History of the Miners' Federation*, p. 20.

7   Ross, *A History of the Miners' Federation*, p. 22.

8   Ross, *A History of the Miners' Federation*, p. 23.

9   Quoted in R. Gollan, *The Coalminers of New South Wales: A History of the Union, 1860–1960*, Melbourne University Press, 1963, p. 41.

10 Ross, *A History of the Miners' Federation*, p. 29.

11 Quoted in John Niland, 'In Search of Shorter Hours: the 1861 and 1874 Iron Trades Disputes', *Labour History*, no. 12, May 1967, p. 12.

12 Niland, 'In Search of Shorter Hours', p. 14.

13 Quoted in Ross, *A History of the Miners' Federation*, pp. 33, 34.

14 M. Waters, *Strikes in Australia: a Sociological Analysis of Industrial Conflict*, Sydney, Allen & Unwin, 1982, p. 88.

15 A. Curthoys, 'Conflict and Consensus: The Seamen's Strike of 1878', in A. Curthoys and A. Markus (eds.), *Who Are Our Enemies?*

16 See R. Markey, *The Making of the Labor Party in New South Wales 1880–1900*, Sydney, NSW University Press, 1988, pp. 146ff.

17 Quoted in J. O'Connor, '1890 – A Turning Point in Labour History: A Reply to Mrs Philipp', *Historical Studies*, vol. 4, no. 16, May 1951, p. 357.

18 Markey, *The Making of the Labor Party*, pp. 136–150; Waters, *Strikes in Australia*, pp. 37–39.

19 Quoted in W.H. Blackmore, R.E. Cotter and M.J. Elliott, *Landmarks: a History of Australia to the Present Day*, Melbourne, Macmillan, 1970, p. 97.

20 Quoted in R. Frances, *The Politics of Work: Gender and Labour in Victoria 1880–1939*, Melbourne, Cambridge University Press, 1993, pp. 35, 36.

21 Quoted in R. Brooks, 'The Melbourne Tailoresses' Strike, 1882–1883: an Assessment', *Labour History*, no. 44, May 1983, p. 30.

22 Brooks, 'The Melbourne Tailoresses' Strike', p. 36.

23 A. Summers, *Damned Whores and God's Police: The Colonisation of Women in Australia*, Melbourne, Penguin, 1975, p. 310.

24 K. Buckley and T. Wheelwright, *No Paradise for Workers: Capitalism and the Common People in Australia 1788–1914*, Melbourne, Oxford University Press, 1988, p. 147.

25 Quoted in Frances, *The Politics of Work*, pp. 33, 34.

26 Quoted in Frances, *The Politics of Work*, p. 35.

27 Quoted in G. Serle, *The Rush to be Rich: a History of the Colony of Victoria 1883–1889*, Melbourne University Press, 1971, pp. 117, 118.

28 Quoted in Fitzpatrick, *A Short History of the Australian Labor Movement*, p. 106.

29 Quoted in Serle, *The Rush to be Rich*, p. 118.

30 Ross, *A History of the Miners' Federation*, p. 64.

31 Quoted in J. Merritt, *The Making of the AWU*, Melbourne, Oxford University Press, 1986, p. 51.

32 Serle, *The Rush to be Rich*, p. 115.

33 Merritt, *The Making of the AWU*, p. 107.

34 *Report of the Royal Commission on Strikes*, p. 52.

35 Quoted in Merritt, *The Making of the AWU*, p. 105.

36 Quoted in Merritt, *The Making of the AWU*, p. 94.

37 Quoted in Buckley and Wheelwright, *No Paradise for Workers*, p. 180.

38 Quoted in Merritt, *The Making of the AWU*, p. 161.

39 W. Nicol, 'Women and the Trade Union Movement in New South Wales: 1890–1900, *Labour History*, no. 36, May 1979, pp. 21 fn, 22.

40 W. Nicol, 'Women and the Trade Union Movement in New South Wales', p. 25.

41 Quoted in Bruce Scates, *A New Australia: Citizenship, Radicalism and the First Republic*, Melbourne, Cambridge University Press, 1997, p 81.

CHAPTER 3

1 Fitzpatrick, *A Short History of the Australian Labor Movement*, p. 113.

2 Svensen, *The Sinews of War*, Chapter 2.

3 Markey, *The Making of the Labor Party*, p. 39.

4 Svensen, *Sinews of War*, p. 88.

5 J. Rickard, *Class and Politics: New South Wales, Victoria and the Early Commonwealth, 1890–1910*, Canberra, ANU Press, 1976, p. 17.

6 Rickard, *Class and Politics*, p. 25.

7 Quoted in Rickard, *Class and Politics*, p. 29.

8 Rickard, *Class and Politics*, p. 23.

9 Quoted in Svenson, *Sinews of War*, p. 129.

10 *Sydney Morning Herald*, 8 September 1890, p. 5.

11 Svensen, *Sinews of War*, pp. 177ff.

12 E. Fosbery, 'The Late Strike: Report of the Inspector General of Police', Legislative Assembly, NSW, *Votes and Proceedings*, Session 1890, vol. 7, p. 628.

13 Quoted in Merritt, *The Making of the AWU*, p. 167.

14 *Sydney Morning Herald*, 24 July 1890, p. 7.

15 Quoted in Rickard, *Class and Politics*, p. 37.

16 Quoted in Fitzpatrick, *A Short History of the Australian Labour Movement*, p. 133.

17 H. Lawson, 'Freedom on the Wallaby', *The Worker* (Brisbane), 16 May 1891, p. 8.

18 Quoted in Merritt, *The Making of the AWU*, p. 260.

19 Scates, *A New Australia*, p. 153.

20 Scates, *A New Australia*, p. 158.

21 Scates, *A New Australia*, p. 164.

22 Scates, *A New Australia*, p. 159.

23 On both socialism and the Labor Party, see V. Burgmann, *'In our Time':
Socialism and the Rise of Labor, 1885–1905*, Sydney, Allen & Unwin, 1985; and
M. Armstrong, *Origins of the Australian Labor Party*, Melbourne, Socialist
Alternative, 1998.

24 For example, J. Lee, 'A Redivision of Labour: Victoria's Wages Boards in
Action, 1896–1903', *Australian Historical Studies*, vol. 22, no. 88, 1987.

25 L. Walker, unpublished manuscript.

26 Quoted in Markey, *The Making of the Labor Party*, p. 277.

27 Quoted in J. O'Connor, '1890 – A Turning Point in Labour History', p. 362.

28 A. Gramsci, *Soviets in Italy*, Nottingham, Institute for Workers' Control,
1965, pp. 9, 17.

29 Quoted by D. Plowman, 'Forced March: The Employers and Arbitration', in
S. Macintyre and R. Mitchell (eds.), *Foundations of Arbitration*, p. 138.

30 Quoted in S. Macintyre, 'Neither Capital nor Labour: The Politics of the
Establishment of Arbitration', in S. Macintyre and R. Mitchell (eds.),
Foundations of Arbitration, p. 196.

31 Quoted by Macintyre, 'Neither Capital nor Labour', p. 194.

CHAPTER 4

1 B. Kingston, *My Wife, My Daughter, and Poor Mary Ann: Women and Work
in Australia*, Melbourne, Nelson, 1977, pp. 24–5.

2 D. Deacon, *Managing Gender: the State, the New Middle Class and Women
Workers 1830–1930*, Melbourne, Oxford University Press, 1989, p. 67.

3 Deacon, *Managing Gender*.

4 L. Dale, *The Rural Context of Masculinity and the 'Woman Question': An
Analysis of the Amalgamated Shearers' Union Support for Women's Equality,
NSW, 1890–1895*, Melbourne, Monash Publications in History, No. 8, 1991,
pp. 10, 47.

5 Information on wages from Buckley and Wheelwright, *No Paradise for
Workers*, pp. 141ff.

6 Kingston, *My Wife, My Daughter, and Poor Mary Ann*, p. 58.

7 M. Aveling and J. Damousi (eds.), *Stepping out of History: Documents of
Women at Work in Australia*, Sydney, Allen & Unwin, 1991, pp. 58–9.

8   G. Davison, *The Rise and Fall of Marvellous Melbourne*, Melbourne University Press, 1978, p. 60.
9   See W.A. Sinclair, 'Women and Economic Change in Melbourne 1871–1921', *Historical Studies*, vol. 20, no. 79, 1982; and S. Fitzgerald, *Rising Damp: Sydney 1870–1890*, Melbourne, Oxford University Press, 1987, p. 112.
10 Aveling and Damousi, *Stepping out of History*, p. 72.
11 Kingston, *My Wife, My Daughter, and Poor Mary Ann*, p. 77.
12 Deacon, *Managing Gender*.
13 Baker, *Communicators and their First Trade Unions*, pp. 74.
14 Deacon, *Managing Gender*, pp. 153–154.
15 This is how it's generally treated by Kingston, *My Wife, My Daughter, and Poor Mary Ann*, throughout. Some writers refer to 'feminist' currents, but we should note that the term 'feminism' wasn't current in the late 19th century. I have sometimes used it for convenience, but more cautiously than most. To extend it to those who saw class struggle as the way forward, such as Emma Miller, would be more than a minor, harmless anachronism; it would seriously misrepresent the social and political realities of the time.
16 Moss, *Sound of Trumpets*, p. 195.
17 K. Spearritt, 'New Dawns: First Wave Feminism 1880–1914', in K. Saunders and R. Evans (eds.), *Gender Relations in Australia: Domination and Negotiation*, Sydney, Harcourt Brace Jonanovich, 1992, p. 333.
18 See A. Oldfield, *Woman Suffrage in Australia: A Gift or a Struggle*, Melbourne, Cambridge University Press, 1992, p. 183.
19 S. Petrow, 'Creating an Orderly Society: The Hobart Municipal Police 1880–1898,' *Labour History*, no. 75, November 1998, p. 185.
20 M. Hogan, *The Sectarian Strand: Religion in Australian History*, Ringwood, Penguin, 1987, pp. 145ff; K. Daniels (ed.), *So Much Hard Work: Women and Prostitution in Australian History*, Sydney, Fontana, 1984.
21 B. Searle, *Silk and Calico: Class, Gender and the Vote*, Sydney, Hale and Iremonger, 1988, p. 63.
22 Searle, *Silk and Calico*, p. 22.
23 Oldfield, *Woman Suffrage in Australia*, p. 194.
24 Spearrit, 'New Dawns', p. 341.
25 Merrit, *The Making of the AWU*, p. 108.

26 F.K. Crowley, *A Documentary History of Australia, Vol. 2, Colonial Australia, 1841–1874*, Melbourne, Thomas Nelson, 1980, p. 578.

27 Searle, *Silk and Calico*, pp. 13, 18.

28 Verity Burgmann, 'In our Time', p. 189.

29 R. Evans, K. Saunders and K. Cronin, *Race Relations in Colonial Queensland, A History of Exclusion, Exploitation and Extermination*, St Lucia, University of Queensland Press, 1988, p. 313.

30 A.T. Yarwood and M.J. Knowling, *Race Relations in Australia: A History*, Sydney, Methuen Australia, 1982, p. 172.

31 P. Grimshaw et al., *Creating a Nation*, Melbourne, McPhee Gribble, 1994, p. 192.

32 Oldfield, *Woman Suffrage in Australia*, p. 23.

33 Grimshaw et al., *Creating a Nation*, p. 168; Lee, 'A Redivision of Labour', p. 366.

34 Deacon, *Managing Gender*, p. 178.

35 L. Ollif, *Louisa Lawson: Henry Lawson's Crusading Mother*, Sydney, Rigby, 1978, p. 55; Markey, *The Making of the Labor Party*, p. 206.

36 Deacon, *Managing Gender*, pp. 263–4 fn.

37 *Official Record of the Debates of the Australian Federal Convention*, Adelaide, 1897, p. 722.

38 Oldfield, *Woman Suffrage in Australia*, p. 31.

39 See Oldfield, *Woman Suffrage in Australia*, pp. 71–2.

40 Oldfield, *Woman Suffrage in Australia*, p. 82.

41 Oldfield, *Woman Suffrage in Australia*, p. 221.

42 J. Damousi, *Women Come Rally: Socialism, Communism and Gender in Australia, 1890–1955*, Melbourne, Oxford University Press, 1994, p. 35.

43 Scates, *A New Australia*, pp. 173ff.; the quote is on p. 181.

44 Scates, *A New Australia*, pp. 193ff; the quote is on p. 200.

CHAPTER 5

1 D.B. Rose, 'The Saga of Captain Cook: Morality in Aboriginal and European Law', *Australian Aboriginal Studies*, no. 2, 1984, pp. 25–35.

2   H. Goodall, *Invasion to Embassy: Land in Aboriginal Politics in New South Wales, 1770–1872*, Sydney, Allen & Unwin, 1996, pp. 11–12.

3   H. Reynolds, *The Other Side of the Frontier: an Interpretation of the Aboriginal Response to the Invasion and Settlement of Australia*, Townsville, James Cook University, p. 119.

4   Reynolds, *The Other Side of the Frontier*, pp. 62–63.

5   Quoted in Grimshaw et al., *Creating a Nation*, p. 22.

6   L. Robson, *A History of Tasmania*, Vol 1, *Van Diemen's Land from the Earliest Times to 1855*, Melbourne, Oxford University Press, 1983, p. 260.

7   Eric Hobsbawm, quoted in Reynolds, *The Other Side of the Frontier*, pp. 180, 193.

8   C. Wise, 'Black Rebel: Musquito', in E. Fry (ed.), *Rebels & Radicals*, Sydney, Allen & Unwin, 1983, p. 4.

9   Robson, *A History of Tasmania*, Vol. 1, p. 227.

10 Quoted in Henry Reynolds, *Frontier: Aborigines, Settlers and Land*, Sydney, Allen & Unwin, 1987, p. 22.

11 James Miller, *Koori: A Will to Win*, Sydney, Angus & Robertson, 1985, p. 51.

12 Quoted in Reynolds, *The Other Side of the Frontier*, pp. 56–57.

13 Quoted in Reynolds, *The Other Side of the Frontier*, p. 119.

14 Both quotes in Reynolds, *The Other Side of the Frontier*, p. 117.

15 Quoted in Reynolds, *The Other Side of the Frontier*, pp. 117, 118.

16 Michael Hogan, *The Sectarian Strand: Religion in Australian History*, Ringwood, Penguin, 1987, p. 121.

17 Yarwood and Knowling, *Race Relations in Australia*, p. 173.

18 Quoted in Goodall, *Invasion to Embassy*, p. 106.

19 Burgmann, 'Capital and Labour'; and 'Writing Racism out of History', *Arena*, no. 67, 1984.

20 P. Griffiths, 'The making of White Australia: Ruling Class agendas, 1876–1888, Ph.D. Thesis, Australian National University, 2006.

21 A. Curthoys, *Race and ethnicity: a study of the response of British colonists to Aborigines, Chinese and non-British Europeans in New South Wales, 1856–1881*, Ph.D. thesis, Macquarie University, 1973, p. 92.

22 Griffiths, 'The making of White Australia'.

23 Curthoys, 'Race and ethnicity'.

24 J. Small, 'Reconsidering White Australia: Class and Anti-Chinese Racism in the 1873 Clunes Riot', Honours Thesis, La Trobe University, 1997, pp. 16, 20 and 60ff.

25 N. Meaney, '"The Yellow Peril": Invasion Scare Novels and Australian Political Culture', in K. Stewart (ed.), *The 1890s: Australian Literature and Literary Culture*, St Lucia, University of Queensland Press, 1996, p. 239.

26 On gold yields, see G. Serle, *The Golden Age: a History of the Colony of Victoria 1851–1868*, Melbourne University Press, 1963, pp. 390–92. The quote is in Yarwood and Knowling, *Race Relations in Australia*, p. 165.

27 Burgmann, 'Capital and Labor', pp. 31–32.

28 Andrew Markus, *Fear and Hatred: Purifying Australia and California 1850–1901*, Sydney, Hale and Iremonger, 1979, p.183.

29 Small, 'Reconsidering White Australia', pp. 69ff.

30 Markus, *Fear and Hatred*, p. 20.

31 H. McPherson, *To Stand Truly By Each Other: the Eureka Rebellion and the Continuing Struggle for Democracy*, Sydney, Bookmarks, 2004, pp. 38–39.

32 Markus, *Fear and Hatred*, p. 19; K. Cronin, *Colonial Casualties: Chinese in Early Victoria*, Melbourne University Press, 1982, p. 59.

33 Crowley, 'Working Class Conditions in Australia, 1788–1851', p. 344.

34 Markus, *Fear and Hatred*, p. 165.

35 Markey, *The Making of the Labor Party*, p. 290.

36 D. Hunt, 'Exclusivism and Unionism: Europeans in the Queensland Sugar Industry 1900–10', in A. Curthoys and A. Markus, *Who Are Our Enemies?* p. 85.

37 Quoted in Evans, Saunders and Cronin, *Race Relations in Colonial Queensland*, p. 285.

38 A. Markus, 'Talka Longa Mouth', *Labour History*, no. 35, Sydney, 1978, p. 140.

39 M. Armstrong, 'Aborigines: Problems of Race and Class', in R. Kuhn and T. O'Lincoln (eds.), *Class and Class Conflict in Australia*, Melbourne, Longman Australia, 1996, p. 68.

40 Quoted in M. Langton, 'In reply to Germaine Greer's Quarterly Essay, "Whitefella Jump Up: The shortest way to nationhood"', *Quarterly Essay*. https://www.quarterlyessay.com.au/correspondence/1225

41 W.G. McMinn, *Nationalism and Federalism in Australia*, Melbourne, Oxford University Press, 1994, p. 199.

42 C. Knapman, 'Reproducing Empire: Exploring Ideologies of Gender and Race on Australia's Pacific Frontier', in S. Margarey, S. Rowley and S. Sheridan (eds.), *Debutante Nation: Feminism Contests the 1890s*, Sydney, Allen & Unwin, 1993, pp. 127–8.

43 Quoted in H. McQueen, *A New Britannia: an Argument concerning the Social Origins of Australian Radicalism and Nationalism*, Melbourne, Penguin, 1986, pp. 18–19.

44 B. Penny, 'The Australian Debate on the Boer War', *Historical Studies*, vol. 14, no. 56, April 1971, p. 541.

45 Quoted in McQueen, *A New Britannia*, p. 107.

46 See T. O'Lincoln, *The Neighbour from Hell: Two Centuries of Australian Imperialism*, Melbourne, Interventions, 2021.

47 M. Armstrong, *The Origins of the Australian Labor Party*.

BIBLIOGRAPHY AND FURTHER READING ON COLONIAL AUSTRALIA

This section lists works cited in this
book and other titles of interest to readers
on aspects of the period.

Alford, K., 'Gilt-Edged Women: Women and Mining in Colonial Australia', *Working Papers in Economic History*, no. 64, Canberra, ANU, 1986.

Alford, K., *Production or Reproduction*, Melbourne, Oxford University Press, 1984.

Allen, J., 'The Making of a Prostitute Proletariat in Early Twentieth Century New South Wales', in K. Daniels (ed.), *So Much Hard Work: Women and Prostitution in Australian History*, pp. 192–232.

Alomes, S., 'Australian Nationalism in the Eras of Imperialism and "Internationalism"', *Australian Journal of Politics & History*, vol. 34, issue 3, pp. 320–332.

Armstrong, M., *The Origins of the Australian Labor Party*, Melbourne, Socialist Alternative, 1996.

Arnold, J., Spearritt, P. and Walker, D. (eds), *Out of Empire: the British Domination of Australia*, Melbourne, Mandarin, 1993.

Aveling, M. and Damousi, J. (eds.), *Stepping out of History: Documents of Women at Work in Australia*, Sydney, Allen & Unwin, 1991.

Bacchi, C., 'The "Woman Question" in South Australia', in E. Richards (ed.), *The Flinders History of South Australia*, pp. 403–32.

Baker, D.W.A., 'The Origins of Robertson's Land Acts', *Historical Studies*, no. 30, May 1958.

Baker, J.S., *Communicators and their First Trade Unions: a History of the Telegraphist and Postal Clerk Unions of Australia*, Sydney, Union of Postal Clerks and Telegraphists, 1980.

Bell, D., *Daughters of the Dreaming*, Sydney, McPhee Gribble/Allen & Unwin, 1990.

Berzins, B., *The Coming of the Strangers: Life in Australia, 1788–1822*, Sydney, Collins, 1988.

Blainey, G., *A Land Half Won*, Melbourne, MacMillan, 1980.

Bongiorno, F., 'Marxism and the Victorian Labour Movement', in C. Ferrier and R. Pelan (eds.), *The Point of Change: Marxism/Australia/History/Theory*, St Lucia, Australian Studies Centre, Department of English, University of Queensland, 1998, pp. 64–74.

Brooks, R., 'The Melbourne Tailoresses' Strike, 1882–1883: an Assessment', *Labour History*, no. 44, May 1983, pp. 27–38.

Buckley, K.D. (Ken), *The Amalgamated Engineers in Australia, 1852–1920*, Canberra, ANU, 1970.

Buckley, K. and Wheelwright, T., *No Paradise for Workers: Capitalism and the Common People in Australia 1788–1914*, Melbourne, Oxford University Press, 1988.

Burgmann, V., 'Capital and Labour', in A. Curthoys and A. Markus (eds.), *Who Are Our Enemies?* pp. 20–34.

Burgmann, V., *'In our Time': Socialism and the Rise of Labor, 1885–1905*, Sydney, Allen & Unwin, 1985.

Burgman, V., 'Premature Labour: the Maritime Strike and the Parliamentary Strategy', in J. Hagan and A. Wells (eds.), *The Maritime Strike*.

Butler-Bowdon, E., *In the Service? a History of Railway Workers and their Union*, South Yarra, Hyland House, 1991.

Butlin, N.G., *Economics and the Dreamtime: a Hypothetical History*, Melbourne, Cambridge University Press, 1993.

Butlin, N.G., *Forming a Colonial Economy, Australia 1810–1850*, Melbourne, Cambridge University Press, 1994.

Cannon, M., *Australia in the Victorian Age: vol 1, Who's Master? Who's Man?* Melbourne, John Currey O'Neil, 1982; vol 2, *Life in the Country*, Melbourne, Nelson, 1973.

Carboni, R., *The Eureka Stockade*, Melbourne University Press, 1993.

Churchward, L.G. (Lloyd), 'Americans and Other Foreigners at Eureka', *Historical Studies: Australia and New Zealand*, Eureka Centenary Supplement, University of Melbourne, December 1954.

Clark, C.M.H. (Manning), *A History of Australia II, New South Wales and Van Diemen's Land 1822–1838*, Melbourne University Press, 1968.

Connell, R.W., 'The Convict Rebellion of 1804', *Melbourne Historical Journal*, vol. 5, 1965, pp. 27–37.

Connell, R.W. and Irving, T.H., *Class Structure in Australian History: Documents, Narrative and Argument*, Melbourne, Longman Cheshire, 1980.

Cronin, K., *Colonial Casualties: Chinese in Early Victoria*, Melbourne University Press, 1982.

Crowley, F.K., *Working Class Conditions in Australia, 1788–1851*, Ph.D. thesis, Melbourne University, 1949.

Curthoys, A., 'Conflict and Consensus: the Seamen's Strike of 1878', in A. Curthoys and A. Markus (eds.), *Who Are Our Enemies?* pp. 48–65.

Curthoys, A. and Markus, A., *Who Are Our Enemies? Racism and the Working Class in Australia*, Sydney, Hale and Iremonger, in association with the Australian Society for the Study of Labour History, Neutral Bay (NSW), 1978.

Dale, L., 'The Rural Context of Masculinity and the "Woman Question": an Analysis of the Amalgamated Shearers' Union Support for Women's Equality, NSW, 1890–1895', *Monash Publications in History*, no. 8, Melbourne, 1991.

Daniels, K. (ed.), *So Much Hard Work: Women and Prostitution in Australian History*, Sydney, Fontana, 1984.

Daniels, K. and Murnane, M., *Uphill All the Way: a Documentary History of Women in Australia*, St Lucia, University of Queensland Press, 1980.

Davidson, A., *The Invisible State: the Formation of the Australian State 1788–1901*, Melbourne, Cambridge University Press, 1991.

Davies, M., 'Cornish Miners and Class Relations in Early Colonial South Australia: the Burra Burra Strikes of 1848–49', *Historical Studies*, vol. 26, no. 5, October 1995, pp. 568–595.

Davison, G., *The Rise and Fall of Marvellous Melbourne*, Melbourne University Press, 1978.

Deacon, D., *Managing Gender: the State, the New Middle Class and Women Workers 1830–1930*, Melbourne, Oxford University Press, 1989.

Donkin, N., *The Women Were There: Nineteen Women Who Enlivened Australia's History*, Melbourne, Collins Dove, 1988.

Donovan, P.F., 'Australia and the Great London Dock Strike: 1889', *Labour History*, no. 23, November 1972.

Dutton, G., *The Squatters: an Illustrated History of Australia's Pastoral Pioneers*, Melbourne, Viking O'Neil, 1985.

Evans, R., Saunders, K. and Cronin, K., *Race Relations in Colonial Queensland: a History of Exclusion, Exploitation and Extermination*, St Lucia, University of Queensland Press, 1988.

Fisher, S., 'Sydney Women and the Workforce 1870–90', in M. Kelly (ed.), *Nineteenth-Century Sydney: Essays in Urban History*, Sydney University Press, 1978.

Fitzgerald, S., *Rising Damp: Sydney 1870–1890*, Melbourne, Oxford University Press, 1987.

Fitzpatrick, B., *British Imperialism and Australia 1973–1833: an Economic History of Australia*, Sydney University Press, 1971.

Fitzpatrick, B., *A Short History of the Australian Labor Movement*, Melbourne, MacMillan, 1968.

Fletcher, B., *Colonial Australia Before 1850*, Melbourne, Nelson, 1986.

Foster, S.G., 'Aboriginal Rights and Official Morality', *The Push from the Bush*, no. 11, November 1981.

Frances, R., *The Politics of Work: Gender and Labour in Victoria 1880–1939*, Melbourne, Cambridge University Press, 1993.

Fry, E. (ed.), *Rebels & Radicals*, Sydney, Allen & Unwin, 1983.

Fry, K., *Beyond the Barrier: Class Formation in a Pastoral Society, Bathurst 1818–1848*, Bathurst, Crawford House Press, 1993.

Furphy, J., *Such is Life*, Sydney, Angus & Robertson, 1980.

Garden, D., *Victoria: a History*, Melbourne, Nelson, 1984.

Gollan, R., *The Coalminers of New South Wales: a History of the Union, 1860–1960*, Melbourne University Press, 1963.

Gollan, R., *Radical and Working Class Politics: a Study of Eastern Australia 1850–1910*, Melbourne University Press, 1960.

Goodall, H., *Invasion to Embassy: Land in Aboriginal Politics in New South Wales, 1770–1872*, Sydney, Allen & Unwin, 1996.

Goodman, D., *Gold Seeking: Victoria and California in the 1850s*, Sydney, Allen & Unwin, 1994.

Grassby, A. and Marji, J., *Six Australian Battlefields: the Black Resistance of Invasion and the White Struggle Against Colonial Oppression*, Sydney, Angus & Robertson, 1988.

Griffin, J. (ed.), *Essays in Economic History of Australia*, Brisbane, Jacaranda Press, 1970.

Griffiths, P., 'The making of White Australia: Ruling Class agendas, 1876–1888*, Ph.D. Thesis, Australian National University, 2006.

Grimshaw, P. et al., *Creating a Nation*, Melbourne, McPhee Gribble, 1994.

Hagan, J. and Wells, A. (eds.), *The Maritime Strike: a Centennial Retrospective: Essays in Honour of Eric Fry*, Wollongong, Five Islands Press, 1992.

Hirst, J.G., *Convict Society and its Enemies: a History of Early New South Wales*, Sydney, Allen & Unwin, 1983.

Hirst, J.G., *The Strange Birth of Colonial Democracy: New South Wales 1848–1884*, Sydney, Allen & Unwin, 1988.

Hobsbawm, E., *The Forward March of Labour Halted?* London, Verso, 1981.

Hogan, M., *The Sectarian Strand: Religion in Australian History*, Ringwood, Penguin, 1987.

Hughes, H., 'The Eight Hour Day and the Development of the Labour Movement in Victoria in the Eighteen-Fifties', *Historical Studies*, vol. 9, no. 36, 1961, pp. 396–412.

Hughes, R., *The Fatal Shore: a History of the Transportation of Convicts to Australia, 1787–1868*, London, Collins Harvill, 1987.

Hunt, D., 'Exclusivism and Unionism: Europeans in the Queensland Sugar Industry 1900–10', in A. Curthoys and A. Markus (eds.), *Who Are Our Enemies?*, pp. 80–95.

Hunt, S., *Spinifex and Hessian: Women in North-West Australia, 1860–1900*, Perth, University of Western Australia Press, 1986.

Irving, H., *To Constitute a Nation: a Cultural History of Australia's Constitution*, Melbourne, Cambridge University Press, 1997.

Irving, T. (ed.), *Challenges to Labour History*, Sydney, UNSW Press, 1994.

Irving, T., Review of Michael Quinlan, *The Origins of Worker Mobilisation: Australia 1788–1850*, London, Routledge, 2017, in *The Economic and Labour Relations Review*, vol. 29, no. 2, 2018, pp. 263–268.

Irving, T., 'Society and the Language of Class', in N. Meaney (ed.), *Under New Heavens: Cultural Transmission and the Making of Australia*, Melbourne, Heinemann, 1989.

Irving, T., *The Southern Tree of Liberty*, Sydney, Federation Press, 2006.

Kent, B., 'Agitation on the Victorian Gold Fields 1851–4: an Interpretation', *Historical Studies: Australia and New Zealand*, November 1954.

Kiddle, M., *Men of Yesterday: a Social History of the Western District of Victoria, 1834–1890*, Melbourne University Press, 1963.

King, H., *Richard Bourke*, Melbourne, Oxford University Press, 1971.

King, J. (ed.), *The First Settlement: the Convict Village that Founded Australia 1788–90*, Melbourne, MacMillan, 1984.

Kingston, B., *My Wife, My Daughter, and Poor Mary Ann: Women and Work in Australia*, Melbourne, Nelson, 1977.

Knapman, C., 'Reproducing Empire: Exploring Ideologies of Gender and Race on Australia's Pacific Frontier', in S. Margarey, S. Rowley and S. Sheridan (eds.), *Debutante Nation*, pp. 125–35.

Knight, R., *Illiberal Liberal: Robert Lowe in New South Wales, 1842–1850*, Melbourne University Press, 1966.

Kociumbas, J., *The Oxford History of Australia, vol 2, 1770–1860*, Melbourne, Oxford University Press, 1991.

Lawson, H., *While the Billy Boils*, Melbourne, Lloyd O'Neil, 1970.

Lee, J. and Fahey, C. 'A Boom for Whom? Some Developments in the Australian Labour Market, 1870–1891,' *Labour History*, vol. 50, pp. 1–27.

Lockwood, R., *Ship to Shore: a History of Melbourne's Waterfront and Its Union Struggles*, Sydney, Hale & Ironmonger, 1990.

Macintyre, S., 'Neither Capital nor Labour: the Politics of the Establishment of Arbitration', in S. Macintyre and R. Mitchell (eds.), *Foundations of Arbitration*, pp.178–200.

Macintyre, S., *Winners and Losers: the Pursuit of Social Justice in Australian History*, Sydney, Allen & Unwin, 1985.

Macintyre, S. and Mitchell, R. (eds.), *Foundations of Arbitration: the Origins and Effects of State Compulsory Arbitration, 1890–1914*, Melbourne, Oxford University Press, 1989.

Main, J.M., 'Men of Capital', in E. Richards (ed.), *The Flinders History of South Australia*, pp. 96–104.

Margarey, S., Rowley, S. and Sheridan, S. (eds.), *Debutante Nation: Feminism Contests the 1890s*, Sydney, Allen & Unwin, 1993.

Markey, R., *The Making of the Labor Party in New South Wales 1880–1900*, Sydney, NSW University Press, 1988.

Markey, R., 'Trade Unions, the Labor Party and the Introduction of Arbitration in New South Wales and the Commonwealth', in S. Macintyre and R. Mitchell (eds.), *Foundations of Arbitration*, pp. 156–177.

Markus, A., *Fear and Hatred: Purifying Australia and California 1850–1901*, Sydney, Hale and Iremonger, 1979.

Martin, A.W., *Essays in Australian Federation*, Melbourne University Press, 1976.

Martin, G., 'Introduction', in *The Founding of Australia, The Argument About Australia's Origins*, Sydney, Hale and Iremonger, 1978.

Massola, A., *Coranderrk: a History of the Aboriginal Station*, Kilmore, Lowden Publishing Company, 1975.

McMinn, W.G., *Nationalism and Federalism in Australia*, Melbourne, Oxford University Press, 1994.

McPherson, H., *To Stand Truly By Each Other: the Eureka Rebellion and the Continuing Struggle for Democracy*, Sydney, Bookmarks, 2004, pp. 38–39.

McQueen, H., *A New Britannia: an Argument concerning the Social Origins of Australian Radicalism and Nationalism*, Melbourne, Penguin, 1978.

McQuilton, J., *The Kelly Outbreak, 1878–1880: the Geographical Dimension of Social Banditry*, Melbourne University Press, 1979. (About Ned Kelly et al.)

Meaney, N., '"The Yellow Peril": Invasion Scare Novels and Australian Political Culture', in K. Stewart (ed.), *The 1890s*, pp. 228–263.

Merritt, J., *The Making of the AWU*, Melbourne, Oxford University Press, 1986.

Miller, J., *Koori: a Will to Win*, Sydney, Angus & Robertson, 1985.

Molony, J., *Eureka*, Melbourne, Penguin, 1984. (The story of the revolt.)

Moss, J., *Sound of Trumpets: History of the Labour Movement in South Australia*, Adelaide, Wakefield Press, 1985.

Neale, J., *The Cutlass and the Lash: Mutiny and Discipline in Nelson's Navy*, London, Pluto Press, 1985.

Nicholas, S. (ed.), *Convict Workers: Reinterpreting Australia's Past*, Melbourne, Cambridge University Press, 1988.

Nicol, W., 'Women and the Trade Union Movement in New South Wales: 1890–1900', *Labour History*, no. 36, May 1979, pp.18–30.

Niland, J., 'In Search of Shorter Hours: the 1861 and 1874 Iron Trades Disputes', *Labour History*, no. 12, May 1967, pp. 3–15.

Norris, R., *The Emergent Commonwealth: Australian Federation: Expectations and Fulfillment 1889–1910*, Melbourne University Press, 1975.

Norton, J. (ed.), *The History of Capital and Labour in All Lands and Ages*, Sydney, Oceanic Publishing, 1888. (A key data source – about colonial Australia, not 'all lands'.)

Official Record of the Debates of the Australian Federal Convention, Adelaide, 1897.

Ollif, L., *Louisa Lawson: Henry Lawson's Crusading Mother*, Sydney, Rigby, 1978.

O'Connor, J., '1890 – a Turning Point in Labour History: a Reply to Mrs Philipp', *Historical Studies*, vol. 4, no. 16, May 1951.

Oldfield, A., *Woman Suffrage in Australia: a Gift or a Struggle*, Melbourne, Cambridge University Press, 1992.

Oxley, D., *Convict Maids: the Forced Migration of Women to Australia*, Melbourne, Cambridge University Press, 1996.

Pascoe, R., *The Manufacture of Australian History*, Melbourne, Oxford University Press, 1979.

Patmore, G., *Australian Labour History*, Melbourne, Longman Cheshire, 1991.

Petrow, S., 'Creating an Orderly Society: the Hobart Municipal Police 1880–1898,' *Labour History*, no. 75, November 1998, pp. 175–194.

Penny, B., 'The Australian Debate on the Boer War', *Historical Studies*, vol. 14, no. 56, April 1971, pp. 526–545.

Perrot, M., *A Tolerable Good Success: Economic Opportunities for Women in New South Wales 1788–1830*, Sydney, Hale and Iremonger, 1983.

Philipp, J., '1890 – the Turning Point in Labour History?', *Historical Studies*, vol. 4, no. 14, May 1950, pp. 145–154.

Plowman, D., 'Forced March: the Employers and Arbitration', in S. Macintyre and R. Mitchell (eds.), *Foundations of Arbitration*, pp. 135-155.

Pownall, E., *Australian Pioneer Women*, Melbourne, Currey O'Neil, 1981.

Quinlan, M., *Contesting Inequality and Worker Mobilisation: Australia 1851–1880*, New York, Routledge, 2020.

Quinlan, M., 'Early Trade Union Organization in Australia: Three Australian Colonies, 1829–50', *Labour and Industry*, vol. 1, no. 1, October 1987, pp. 69–95.

Quinlan, M., *The Origins of Worker Mobilisation: Australia 1788–1850*, New York, Routledge, 2017.

Report of the Royal Commission on Strikes, NSW, 1891.

Reynolds, H., *Fate of a Free People: a Radical Re-Examination of the Tasmanian Wars*, Melbourne, Penguin, 1995.

Reynolds, H., *Frontier: Aborigines, Settlers and Land*, Sydney, Allen & Unwin, 1987.

Reynolds, H., *The Other Side of the Frontier: an Interpretation of the Aboriginal Response to the Invasion and Settlement of Australia*, Townsville, James Cook University, 1981.

Reynolds, H., *With the White People*, Melbourne, Penguin, 1990.

Richards, E. (ed.), *The Flinders History of South Australia: Social History*, Adelaide, Wakefield Press, 1986.

Rickard, J., *Class and Politics: New South Wales, Victoria and the Early Commonwealth, 1890–1910*, Canberra, ANU Press, 1976.

Rickard, J., 'Loyalties', in J. Arnold, P. Spearritt and D. Walker (eds.), *Out of Empire*, pp. 35–55.

Roberts, S., *Charles Hotham: a Biography*, Melbourne University Press, 1985.

Robinson, F. and York, B., *The Black Resistance*, Maryborough, 1977.

Robson, L., *A History of Tasmania*, Vol 1, *Van Diemen's Land from the Earliest Times to 1855*, Melbourne, Oxford University Press, 1983.

Rose, D.B., 'The Saga of Captain Cook: Morality in Aboriginal and European Law', *Australian Aboriginal Studies*, vol. 2, 1984, pp. 24–39.

Ross, E., *A History of the Miners' Federation of Australia*, Sydney, Australasian Coal and Shale Employees' Federation, 1970.

Rubinstein, B., 'The Top Wealth-Holders of New South Wales in 1830–44', *The Push from the Bush*, no. 8, December 1980, pp. 25–50.

Russell, P. and White, R. (eds.), *Pastiche I: Reflections on Nineteenth Century Australia*, Sydney, Allen & Unwin, 1994.

Salt, A., *These Outcast Women: the Parramatta Female Factory 1821–1848*, Sydney, Hale and Iremonger, 1984.

Saunders, K. and Evans, R. (eds.), *Gender Relations in Australia: Domination and Negotiation*, Sydney, Harcourt Brace Jonanovich, 1992.

Scates, B., *A New Australia: Citizenship, Radicalism and the First Republic*, Melbourne, Cambridge University Press, 1997.

Searle, B., *Silk and Calico: Class, Gender and the Vote*, Sydney, Hale and Iremonger, 1988.

Serle, G., *The Golden Age: a History of the Colony of Victoria 1851–1868*, Melbourne University Press, 1963.

Serle, G., *The Rush to be Rich: a History of the Colony of Victoria 1883–1889*, Melbourne University Press, 1971.

Serle, Geoffrey, 'The Victorian Government's Campaign for Federation, 1883–1889', in A.W. Martin (ed.), *Essays in Australian Federation*, pp. 3–33.

Shaw, A.G.L., *The Economic Development of Australia*, Melbourne, Longman, 1969.

Sinclair, W.A., 'Women and Economic Change in Melbourne 1871–1921', *Historical Studies*, vol. 20, no. 79, 1982, pp. 278–291.

Small, J., *Reconsidering White Australia: Class and Anti-Chinese Racism in the 1873 Clunes Riot*, BA Honours thesis, La Trobe University, 1997.

Smith, B., *A Cargo of Women: Susannah Watson and the Convicts of the Princess Royal*, Sydney, NSW University Press, 1988.

Spearritt, K., 'New Dawns: First Wave Feminism 1880–1914', in K. Saunders and R. Evans (eds.), *Gender Relations in Australia: Domination and Negotiation*, pp. 325–349.

Stewart, K. (ed.), *The 1890s: Australian Literature and Literary Culture*, St Lucia, University of Queensland Press, 1996.

Summers, A., *Damned Whores and God's Police: the Colonisation of Women in Australia*, Melbourne, Penguin, 1975.

Summers, J., 'Colonial Race Relations', in E. Richards (ed.), *The Flinders History of South Australia*.

Svensen, S., *The Shearers' War: the Story of the 1891 Shearers' Strike*, St Lucia, University of Queensland Press, 1989.

Svensen, S., *The Sinews of War: Hard Cash and the 1890 Maritime Strike*, Sydney, University of NSW Press, 1995.

Tanner, L., 'A Protracted Evolution: Labor in Victorian Politics 1889–1903', *Labour History*, no. 42, May 1982, pp. 40–53.

Terry, D.H.M., *The Development of the Labour Movement in New South Wales 1833–46*, MA thesis, Sydney University, 1951.

Thomas, L., *The Development of the Labour Movement in the Sydney District of New South Wales*, Canberra, Australian Society for the Study of Labour History, (reprint of MA Thesis, Sydney University, 1919), 1962.

Thompson, R., *Australian Imperialism in the Pacific: the Expansionist Era 1820–1920*, Melbourne University Press, 1980.

Thorpe, B., *Colonial Queensland: Perspectives on a Frontier Society*, St Lucia, University of Queensland Press, 1996.

Trainor, L., *British Imperialism and Australian Nationalism: Manipulation, Conflict and Compromise in the Late Nineteenth Century*, Melbourne, Cambridge University Press, 1994.

Turner, I., *Room for Manoeuvre: Writings on History, Politics, Ideas and Play*, Richmond, Drummond, 1982.

Walshe, R.D., 'The Significance of Eureka in Australian History', *Historical Studies*, Eureka Centenary Supplement, University of Melbourne, December 1954.

Waters, M., *Strikes in Australia: a Sociological Analysis of Industrial Conflict*, Sydney, Allen & Unwin, 1982.

Whitaker, A-M., *Unfinished Revolution: United Irishmen in New South Wales 1800–1810*, Sydney, Crossing Press, 1994.

Windschuttle, E. (ed.), *Women, Class and History, Perspectives on Australia 1788–1978*, Melbourne, Fontana/Collins, 1980.

Wise, C., 'Black Rebel: Musquito', in Fry, E. (ed.), *Rebels and Radicals*.

Yarwood, A.T. and Knowling, M.J., *Race Relations in Australia: a History*, Sydney, Methuen Australia, 1982.

UNITED WE STAND

IMAGE CREDITS

Abbreviations

ANU	Australian National University Library
NLA	National Library of Australia
SLNSW	State Library of New South Wales
SLQ	State Library of Queensland
SLSA	State Library of South Australia
SLV	State Library of Victory
UQ	The University of Queensland

p. 12   SLSA (Record Identifier: B 75028, Burra Collection]

pp. 16-17   Drawing: Edward Blackhouse. SLNSW (Record identifier: YEGmyGjn, Dixson Library)

p. 23   *The Guardian* (Sydney, NSW : 1844) 16 March 1844: 1. Web. 14 Feb 2024 <http://nla.gov.au/nla.news-page22332887>

p. 26   Photo: Charles Nettleton. SLV (Record identifier: 9918054293607636)

p. 31   Photo: Terrance McGann. SLSA (Record identifier: B 45731, Acre 350 Collection)

p. 37   SLNSW (Record identifier: 1kVd5Oxn)

p. 40   Photo: Samuel White Sweet. SLSA (Record identifier: 43158, Sweet Collection)

p. 49	ANU, (Record identifier: K3191, Noel Butlin Archives Centre)
p. 65	SLNSW, (Record identifier: PXD 993, Mort family pictorial material and realia, 1857-1910, Mitchell Library)
p. 66	Cartoon depicting women assaulting strikebreakers. Image reproduced with kind permission of Outback Archives, Broken Hill City Library, NSW.
p. 67	SLQ (Record identifier: 99183798374902061, John Oxley Library)
p. 69	NLA (Record identifier: 1554871)
p. 72	SLQ (Record identifier: 99183505879202061, John Oxley Library)
p. 83	NLA (Record identifier: 29791, T. Humphrey & Co.)
p. 90	SLQ (Record identifier: 13414702061, John Oxley Library)
p. 93	Weekly Herald (South Australia) 13 November 1896. Accessed at https://www.centreofdemocracy.sa.gov.au/%EF%BB%BFsuffrage-125-working-women-in-the-nineteenth-century/
p. 100	SLV (Record identifier: 9939655060307636)
pp. 104-5	Photo: Areas Photographic Company. SLV (Record identifier: 9937095843607636)
p. 111	Photo: Samuel White Sweet. SLSA (Record identifier: PRG 742/5/90)
p. 112	UQ (Record Identifier: UQFL89, eSpace McConnel Family Collection)
p. 119	SLV (Record identifier: 939654238007636, David Syme & Co)
p. 122	'Islander labourers' https://www.nma.gov.au/defining-moments/resources/islander-labourers
p. 124	SLQ (Record identifier: 99183513417802061, John Oxley Library)
p. 166	Photographer Janey Stone

INDEX

Adelaide 47, 65, 88

Amalgamated Miners' Association 38, 47-48

Australian Shearers' Union 48-52

Arbitration 36, 38, 47, 62, 65, 73-80

Arthur, Governor 5, 15

Australian Agricultural Company 5, 34-35, 59

Australian Labor Federation 52, 57

Australian Socialist League 63, 101

Australian Union Benefit Society (AUBS) 19-20

Australian Workers' Union (AWU) 51, 68-69, 77, 94, 127, 130, 135-136, 138, 149

Ballarat (Vic) 32, 48, 121

Barcaldine 32, 67, 72

Barton, Edmond 127-128

Beath, Schiess and Co. 43

Bendigo (Vic) 47, 121

BHP 48, 69-70

Bigge, Commissioner 4-5

Boer War 129, 142, 150

Boot and Shoemakers, Boot Trade Union, Bootmakers 10, 12, 27, 45- 46, 53-54

Bourke (NSW) 50, 122, 127

Brisbane 39, 65, 112, 118, 136, 146

Broken Hill 48, 65-66, 69, 76, 104-105

Burra Burra mine 12-13, 133, 145

Cairns (Qld) 125

Charters Towers 126

Chinese 39, 71, 75, 95, 115-127, 140, 141, 145, 152

Clermont (Qld) 67-68

Clunes (Vic) 120-121, 141, 152

Clunes Miners' Association 121

Coal industry 34-35, 38, 48, 59, 99

Coal miners 29, 34, 38, 47, 60, 76, 134, 146, 151

Cook, James 102, 107,139, 140, 151

Cooper, Leontine 101

Damousi, Joy 137, 138, 139, 143

Darling Downs 52

Darling, Governor 5

Deakin, Alfred 61, 80

Duncan, William 20-22

Eight hour day 29, 31-33, 36, 43-44, 126, 134, 147

Employers' organisations 15, 79, 46-47, 57-65, 70, 78, 80

Engineers 10, 15, 33, 53, 56, 144

Factory Acts 73-74

Fawkner, John Pascoe 118

Federation 74, 95, 96, 116, 127, 130, 134, 148, 149, 151

Female Employees' Society 53

Feminism, feminist 2, 44, 91, 92, 93, 94, 138, 142, 148, 152

Ferris, Lizzie 97

First Fleet 4

Fitzpatrick, Brian 1,55, 131, 135-136, 146

Frances, Raelene 44-45, 75, 135, 146

Fruitpickers' Case 79

INDEX

Garment trade 42

Geelong 32

Gender iv, vi, 44, 75, 79, 81, 82, 84, 95-96, 98-99, 103, 128, 135, 137-139, 142, 145, 146, 148, 151, 152

Gilmore, Mary 88

Gipps, Governor 6, 20, 24

Gold mining 13, 29, 34, 38, 114, 120-121, 133, 141,146, 147

Goldstein, Vida 88, 92, 98, 100, 102

Gregson, Jesse 59

Griffiths, Phil 117, 140, 146

Harding, George Rogers 68

Harvester Judgement 79

Higgins, Justice 79

Hill, Alexander 96

Hindmarsh (SA) 27

Hipkiss, Richard 19-20

Hobart 16, 25, 109, 138, 158

Hobart Town Trades' Union 25

Houses of Call 10

Howard, John 1

Hughes, Billy 79, 134, 147

Hunter Valley 34-35

Hunter, Governor 4

Hutt, Governor 113

Immigration Restriction Act 128

Imperialism 115, 118, 128-129, 142, 146, 152

Indigenous people 107-117, 140, 153
- Kinship systems 109
- Protection Board 114
- Relation to land 107-109, 112
- Resistance 110-111

Inter-colonial unionism 39, 41, 47, 60

Irish 82, 92, 114-115, 130

Japan 115

Jondaryan station 52, 56-57, 59

Kernot, Professor 47

Kinchela (NSW) 114

Kingston, Beverley 81, 137, 138, 148

Lambing Flat 95, 118,120

Lane, William 101, 103

Lang, J.D. 18

Launceston (Tas) 25

Launceston Working Men's Association 25

Lawson, Henry 129, 136, 139,148,149

Lawson, Louisa 88, 93, 96-97, 139, 149

Lee, Mary 91, 100

Lindsay, Con 103

Lipscombe, Nathaniel 20

Locke, Lilian 88

Macarthur, Elizabeth 5

Macarthur, Hannibal 8

Macdermott, Henry 20, 22

Macquarie, Governor 3, 4

Mair, George 51

Mair, John 58

Marine Officers' Association 56-57, 60

Maritime strike 56- 62, 65, 66, 69, 130, 144, 147, 152

Maritime unions 1, 52, 60

Marriage 82, 92-93, 103

Master and Servant Act 25, 27

McEachern, James 20, 23

Melbourne 7, 9, 16, 29, 31, 32, 36, 39, 46, 47, 54, 59, 61, 67, 82, 86, 118, 120, 132-133, 145

INDEX

Mildura Land and Labour Union 53

Miller, Emma 91, 138

Mitchell, Thomas 111

Montefiore, Dora 89

Moree (NSW) 48

Morisset, James Thomas 5

Moroney, Jamie 76

Mort's Dock 36

Mt Kembla 65

Murray River 108

Musquito 110, 140, 153

Mutual Protection Association (MPA) 22-24

New South Wales 3, 5, 6, 13, 15, 19, 24, 27, 29, 33, 35, 38, 48, 50, 52, 56, 58, 64, 73, 76, 78, 82, 86, 89, 93, 95, 97, 111, 112, 114, 118, 120, 122, 128, 132-134, 136, 143, 145, 146-153

New unionism 38-39, 45, 83

New Zealand 29, 33, 47, 48, 49

Newcastle 33, 34-35, 39

Nichols, G.L. 21

Nurses 84, 86, 88

Orange Lodges 115

Outwork 42, 45-46, 85, 98

P.N. Russell and Co. 33, 36-37

Pacific Islanders 115, 122, 123, 125

Pacific Island Labourers Act 128

Parkes, Clarinda 82

Parkes, Henry 61, 73, 76, 82, 101, 118, 124

Patriotic Association 19, 20

Port Phillip Patriot 18

Post offices 83, 86, 97

Prendergast, George 74

Price, Tom 62

Prince Alfred 114

Queensland 52, 57, 66-69, 87, 91, 93, 101, 113, 119, 125, 127, 139, 141, 145, 147, 152

Queensland Women's Suffrage League 93

Racism vi, 2, 95, 97, 114, 116-118, 121, 123-130, 133, 140, 141, 145, 152

Railways 34, 39, 48, 52, 76

Reid, George 76

Riverina 48, 50

Rodney (ship) 68

Royal Commissions 51, 73, 82, 95, 135, 150

Rum Corps 3

Salvation Army 71, 93

Sandridge (Port Melbourne) 46

Scates, Bruce 103, 136, 137, 139, 151

Scott, Rose 89, 91, 92, 10

Seafarers 39, 4

Searle, Betty 94, 138, 139, 151

Selectors (small farmers) 20, 83, 120, 126-127

Settlement or invasion? 110-112

Sexuality 92, 95, 115, 128

Shearers 39, 41, 48-52, 57, 64-69, 76, 83, 123, 137, 145, 152

Sheep 67, 110, 112-113

Smith, Bruce 46-47

Socialists 61, 102, 103, 106

Society of Emigrant Mechanics 19

South Australia 9, 13, 14, 24-27, 32, 48, 59, 68, 89, 91, 99, 111, 133, 143, 145, 148-150, 152

South Australian Political Association 27

Spence, Catherine 86

Spence, William Guthrie 39, 42, 47, 48, 51, 52, 57, 59, 60, 69, 83, 84

Squatters 20, 21, 24, 63, 101, 145

Stanley, Creo 53, 103

Star and Workingman's Guardian 17

Stephen, James 117

Stephens, George 85

Stevenson, Robert 127

Stirling, Edward 88

Storey, J.H. 65

Straiter, James 8

Strikes vi, 9-11, 13-14, 34, 38, 41, 45-48, 51, 53, 55, 60, 71, 73, 77, 98, 102, 120, 122, 126, 132-135, 145, 150, 153

Suffrage 18, 27, 81, 88-94, 96-102, 115, 138-139, 150

Summers, Anne 44, 135, 152

Summerville, Rose 54

Sutherland, Benjamin 23

Svensen, Stuart 55, 57, 136, 152

Sweating 44, 73, 74

Sydney 5, 7-12, 15, 18-21, 24, 29, 36, 39, 52-54, 63, 65, 83, 88, 109, 114, 118, 132-133, 146, 151, 152

Sydney Gazette 8

Tailoresses 43-45, 53-54, 135, 144

Tasmania 9, 14, 24-25, 48, 49, 91, 110, 140, 151

Teachers 97, 84, 86, 88, 97

Telegraphers 87, 132, 144

Terra nullius 116

The Argus 50, 121

The Australian 132

The Dawn 93, 96

The Empire 118

The Guardian 17, 22-24, 132

The Hummer 127

The Transmitter 87

The Worker 54, 95, 129, 136

Trades and Labour Councils 36-37, 53-54, 65, 76, 123

Trades Hall (Victoria) 43, 45, 46, 61, 64, 74

Trenwith, W.A. 45, 65, 71

Tarenorerer (Walyer) 110

Tyler, Peter 11, 15

Typographers 8-9, 10, 53

Typographers' Journal 103

Unemployed 24, 35, 47, 61, 70-71, 78, 125

Unions, craft 10, 39, 41, 42, 52, 82, 84, 97

Van Diemens Land 5, 7, 9, 110, 140, 144, 151

Victoria 29, 35, 38, 42, 48, 50, 56, 58, 61, 68, 73, 76, 77, 82, 87, 91, 92, 118, 119, 120, 121, 134-136, 141, 145-147, 151

Victorian Employers' Union 58

Victorian Women's Post and Telegraph Association 97

Wages Boards 73-74, 78-80, 137

Wagga Wagga (NSW) 48

Wakefield, Edward Gibbon 14, 24

Warfare on the frontier 109-110, 120

Waterside workers 8, 45, 60

Wells, George 27

Wentworth, W.C. 18-19

Western Australia 9, 24, 113

Westgarth, William 118

Wharf Labourers' Union 46, 79

Wheelwright, Ted 44, 135, 137, 144

White Australia 28, 95, 114-130

Williamstown (Vic) 46, 63

Windeyer, Mary 89

Winship, J.B. 35

Women workers 53-54, 75, 98

Women's Christian Temperance Union (WCTU) 89-92, 100

Women's Liberation Movement 94

Working Men's Association (South Australia) 27

Working Men's Association (Tasmania) 25
Working Women's Trade Union 89, 91
Yota-Yota (Yorta-Yorta) clan 108

TOM O'LINCOLN AT LAUNCH OF FIRST EDITION OF *UNITED WE STAND* 2005

TOM O'LINCOLN
LEGACY PROJECT

Tom O'Lincoln was born in California in 1947. He grew up in Walnut Creek, east of San Francisco, and attended the University of California, Berkeley. His experiences as an exchange student at the University of Göttingen in 1967–68 had a major impact on the direction of his life. Tom was radicalised and became an activist and a Marxist. In late 1969, he joined the Berkeley branch of the International Socialists (I.S.). In 1971, together with Janey Stone, he came to Australia. In 1972, he became involved in revolutionary politics in this country, a commitment that lasted all his life.

Starting with the small grouping, the Marxist Workers Group, which became Socialist Workers' Action Group at the end of 1972, Tom was a leader and member of various formations which carried through the I.S. tradition, finally joining Socialist Alternative in 2003. Tom was an activist in many political movements and an active trade unionist as a teacher and in the public service.

Always a keen traveller, Tom witnessed major struggles in Germany, Portugal and Indonesia; he engaged with socialists and activists in countries as far apart as Nicaragua, Peru, Lebanon, Poland, South Korea and the Philippines. He corresponded with, and met, leading socialists in the UK, the USA, Germany and elsewhere. His language skills enhanced this experience – Tom could conduct political discussions in German, Russian, Spanish (with some excursions into Portuguese, French and Croatian) and, later in life, Indonesian.

Tom was a prolific writer. He wrote extensively for left-wing newspapers, magazines and websites, including his own website, which he managed for many years. Tom also translated political material into Indonesian and helped to run an Indonesian language website for 10 years.

Tom's political interests were always very wide. Having settled here, he made Australia his focus. He published books on Australian history, Australian imperialism, the Communist Party of Australia, the left and social struggles. He contributed works on many international topics, with Indonesia being a special interest during the 1990s. He also wrote on Marxist theory and economics, Stalinism and other theoretical subjects. A list of all Tom's longer works is included in *The Expropriators are Expropriated*.

Unfortunately, following a diagnosis of Parkinson's disease in 2012, Tom found it increasingly difficult to continue the creative process. He published the last two of his books with help from others. For several years, Tom lived in an aged care facility, where he continued his interest in current events and the development of politics in the world. He died on 13 October 2023.

Some of Tom's books were published with the help of Vulgar Press. Generally, although various imprints were named, they were effectively self-published, mostly with funds from the Jeff Goldhar Project. When Interventions was set up in 2015 as an independent, not-for-profit radical publisher, we took over Tom's backlist.

All the books prior to 2015 were published conventionally, with print runs determined by finances at the time. This led to variable stock levels, not helped by the failure of the main distributor and the disappearance of some stock. As several titles became out of print, Interventions initiated a project of publishing new editions of all Tom's major works, with new design, illustrations and new contextual essays or prefaces. Importantly, these titles are added to print-on-demand services, ensuring that these political ideas will always be accessible. The content of Tom's books has stood the test of time. His is a literary legacy worth preserving and extending to new audiences.

The books that constitute this project are:

1985	*Into the Mainstream: The Decline of Australian Communism*
1993, 2023	*Years of Rage: Social Conflicts in the Fraser Era*
1998, 2022	*Rebel Women in Australian Working Class History* (co-edited with Sandra Bloodworth)
2005, 2024	*United We Stand: Class Struggle in Colonial Australia*
2011	*Australia's Pacific War: Challenging a National Myth*
2014, 2021	*The Neighbour from Hell: Two Centuries of Australian Imperialism*
2016	*'The Expropriators are Expropriated' and other writings on Marxism*
2017	*The Highway is for Gamblers: a Political Memoir*

Most of these are now complete and available on print-on-demand. After the present work, the remaining two titles, *Into the Mainstream* and *Australia's Pacific War*, are planned to be reissued in the near future as resources allow.

Tom was an activist, a revolutionary socialist and a Marxist his whole adult life. In his political memoir, *The Highway is for Gamblers* (Interventions 2017), he writes:

> I have been a Marxist for half a century. In that time I have participated in and been witness to great struggles and momentous historical events. I've had the privilege of standing shoulder to shoulder with selfless fighters around

the world. Those events and the people involved only confirmed in my mind that human liberation can be won through the mass struggles of the working class.

Tom then asks the question, 'Why be a revolutionary socialist today?' His answer? 'It's a life worth living'. We at Interventions want to keep this legacy alive.

ABOUT INTERVENTIONS

Interventions is an independent, not-for-profit, incorporated publisher. We publish left-wing, radical and socialist books by Australian authors. We welcome books which for political or financial reasons are unlikely to be accepted by commercial publishers. Our books cover a wide range of topics including labour history, left-wing politics, radical cultural themes, socialism and Marxism, memoirs, and works about resistance to racism, sexism and all other forms of oppression.

At Interventions we believe radical ideas matter. We want our books to be part of the development of a critical and engaged Australian left.

By highlighting alternative voices, especially those that have been pushed to the margins, we hope to contribute to a greater insight and awareness of the injustices that exist in society, and the many efforts at the grassroots to right these wrongs.

We welcome publishing proposals. If you are interested in submitting a proposal please check out the information for authors on our website https://interventions.org.au/forauthors. If you think your proposal fits our guidelines please follow the submission process outlined there. Please note we are not currently publishing poetry or fiction.

Interventions has no independent source of income and is committed to keeping prices accessible. As bookshops and warehouses close around the world, our future hangs in the balance. By supporting us you will help us keep radical ideas alive and accessible to all. If you would like to support radical publishing in Australia please consider supporting our Patreon. Visit patreon.com/interventions to donate a small amount each month and get some great rewards.

Website: https://interventions.org.au/

Contact us: info@interventions.org.au or use the contact form on the website.

ABOUT THIS BOOK

The Interventions editor and production project managers for this book were Janey Stone and Phillip Whitefield. Tess Lee Ack edited the text of the 1st edition in preparation for this edition. Images were sourced and selected by Phillip Whitefield and Janey Stone, with input from Steph Grigg. Tom Gilchrist assisted with proof reading.

This book was copy edited by Eris Harrison of Effective Editing.

The cover of this book was designed by Stephanie Grigg. Stephanie is a communication designer based in Melbourne. She recently made the jump to book design after many years of magazine and event design.

The interior of this book was designed and laid out by Viktoria Ivanova of Vik Designs. Viktoria is a communication designer in Melbourne. She is a book publishing fiend, runs Spark Publishing Inc (for art-centric left books) and also designs for Victorian Socialists.

MORE FROM TOM O'LINCOLN

Years of Rage: Social Conflicts in the Fraser Era

The 1970s were indeed, years of rage. A furnace of social conflict forged a resistance to the Fraser regime, on multiple fronts. The actions of organised workers were pivotal, along with the social movements against oppression, war, and environmental ruin. Tom O'Lincoln's book, written in 1993, explains why neither capital nor labour were victors. The social temperature may have cooled since Fraser's time, but the outcomes of the stalemate are enduring.

....

Australia's Pacific War: Challenging a National Myth

War is such a nightmare it's hard to believe any war can retain a positive aura for decades. Yet the vast conflict in the Pacific is a shibboleth for Australian politics to this day. Politicians use its appeal to legitimise modern wars. Tom O'Lincoln questions every aspect of this syndrome. He argues that the Pacific War was an imperialist one on both sides and that wartime Australia was riven with class and other social conflicts.

....

The Neighbour from Hell: Two Centuries of Australian Imperialism

The world is complex and volatile, with economic and military competition contributing to unevenness between states. Imperialism has long been the subject of political debates. This book offers an original study of Australia's "boutique imperialism". Far from being servile and passive agents of the United States and Great Britain, Australia's rulers callously seek to extract maximum benefits from calculated interventions in the global capitalist system.

MORE FROM TOM O'LINCOLN

Into the Mainstream:
The Decline of Australian Communism

At the end of World War II, the Communist Party was a major force in Australian working class life. Yet by the 1980s it had diminished to a demoralised rump, and today it's only a memory. *Into the Mainstream* traces the party's decline from an influential movement, plagued by its bureaucratic Stalinist politics, to a shrinking organisation trying desperately to re-invent itself as a radical force, but finally drifting into the political mainstream. The story is set against such historic events as the Cold War, the Sino-Soviet split, and the social radicalisation of the late sixties.

....

The Highway is for Gamblers:
A political memoir
Introduction by Janey Stone

A moving political memoir that is a testament to a life worth living, in the ranks of those fighting for human liberation. It captures the rich political history of the past six decades, written with a pen that burns with indignation against oppression. This is not a nostalgic memoir of reminiscence, but an insight for the activists of tomorrow who hope to change the world.

....

'The Expropriators are Expropriated'
and other writings on Marxism
Edited by Janey Stone, introduced by Rick Kuhn

This book is an anthology of nine short articles written over a 30 year period. It includes five popular presentations of basic Marxist theory and two articles on the topic of the nature of the system in Russia and state capitalism. The other two chapters are on trade unionism – one on the development of the Marxist theory of trade unions from Marx to the Communist International and the other outlines the history of the Communist-led Minority Movement in Australia during the early 1930s.

MORE FROM INTERVENTIONS

The New Theatre: The people, plays and politics behind Australia's radical theatre
Editor: Lisa Milner

For the first time, this unique collection of essays brings the stories of New Theatre branches around Australia, filling a vital space in Australian cultural history. Radical left-wing theatre history tales, told by theatre practitioners, historians, academics and political ratbags, reveal a rich vein of Australia's hidden cultural heritage. New Theatre advocated for freedom and democracy, aiming to activate audiences politically, and create authentic, non-commercial Australian drama by telling the hidden stories about the real lives of working-class people.

Knocking The Top Off: A People's History of Alcohol in Australia
Edited by Alex Ettling and Iain McIntyre

An intoxicating journey through Australia's relationship with alcohol. Featuring short expositions and deep dives into incidents, eras, groups and individuals, this collection provides an alternative history of Australian society and culture from the bottom up. Contributors include Wendy Bacon, Maggie Brady, Rowan Cahill, Bruce Carter, Carol Corless, Daniel A. Elias, Alex Ettling, Gary Foley, Alison Holland, Terry Irving, Phoebe Kelloway, Diane Kirkby, Tanja Luckins, Hamish Maxwell-Stewart, Chris McConville, Lisa Milner, David Nichols, Michael Quinlan, Nick Southall, Jeff Sparrow, Janey Stone and Graham Willett.

Stuff the Accord! Pay up! Workers' Resistance to the ALP-ACTU Accord
By Liz Ross

This book deals with the 1983-1996 ALP-ACTU Accord. This was a landmark program of restructuring Australian capitalism, a social contract between the Australian Council of Trade Unions (ACTU) and the Australian Labor Party (ALP). It pitched worker against worker, destroyed two unions, oversaw one of the greatest transfers of wealth from workers to employers, and gutted union membership and the gains of previous decades. This story of resistance, from the left and workers' perspective, has not been told in full before.

www.ingramcontent.com/pod-product-compliance
Lightning Source LLC
Chambersburg PA
CBHW072003290426
44109CB00018B/2112